EYEWITNESS TRAVEL
PHRASE BOOK
FRENCH

D1011957

DK

REVISED EDITION
DK LONDON
Senior Editor Christine Stroyan
Senior Art Editors Anna Hall, Amy Child
Art Director Karen Self
Associate Publisher Liz Wheeler
Publishing Director Jonathan Metcalf
Proofreading Laurence Larroche, in association with
First Edition Translations Ltd, Cambridge, UK
Senior Pre-Producer Andy Hilliard
Senior Producers Gary Batchelor, Anna Vallarino

DK DELHI

Assistant Editor Sugandha Agarwal
Assistant Art Editors
Anukriti Arora,
Shubham Rastogi
Art Editor Ravi Indiver
Senior Art Editor Chhaya Sajwan
Managing Editor Soma B. Chowdhury
Senior Managing Art Editor
Arunesh Talapatra

Production Manager Pankaj Sharma
Preproduction Managers
Sunil Sharma, Balwant Singh
Senior DTP Designers
Tarun Sharma, Vishal Bhatia,
Neeraj Bhatia, Ajay Verma

First American edition 2008
This revised edition published in 2017 by
DK Publishing,
345 Hudson Street, New York, New York 10014

Copyright © 2008, 2017 Dorling Kindersley Limited
DK, a Division of Penguin Random House LLC
17 18 19 20 10 9 8 7 6 5 4 3 2 1
001–300202–Jun/2017

A catalog record for this book is available from the Library of Congress.
ISBN: 978-1-4654-6267-1

Printed and bound in China

A WORLD OF IDEAS:
SEE ALL THERE IS TO KNOW
www.dk.com

CONTENTS

4 Introduction

8 Essentials

20 Getting Around

42 Eating Out

62 Places to Stay

80 Shopping

110 Sightseeing

120 Sports and Leisure

136 Health

148 Emergencies

158 Menu Guide

167 / **195**
English–French Dictionary
French–English Dictionary

224 Numbers

INTRODUCTION

This book provides all the key words and phrases you are likely to need in everyday situations. It is grouped into themes, and key phrases are broken down into short sections to help you build a wide variety of sentences. A lot of the vocabulary is illustrated to make it easy to remember, and "You may hear" boxes feature questions you are likely to hear. At the back of the book there is a menu guide, listing about 500 food terms, and a 2,000-word two-way dictionary. Numbers are printed on the last page of the book for quick reference.

NOUNS

All French nouns (words for things, people, and ideas) are masculine or feminine. The gender of singular nouns is usually shown by the word for "the": **le** (masculine) and **la** (feminine). These change to **l'** before a vowel. The plural form is **les**. You can look up the gender of words in the French–English dictionary at the back of the book.

ADJECTIVES

Most French adjectives change endings according to whether they describe a masculine or feminine, singular or plural word. In this book the singular masculine form is shown first, followed by the singular feminine form:

I am lost   **Je suis perdu/perdue**.

"YOU"

There are two ways of saying "you" in French: **vous** (polite form and plural) and **tu** (familiar). In this book we have used **vous**, which is normal with people you don't know.

VERBS

Verbs change according to whether they are in the singular or plural. In phrases where this happens, the singular form of the verb is followed by the plural form:

Where is/are...?   **Où se trouve/trouvent...?**

PRONUNCIATION GUIDE

Below each French word or phrase in this book, you will find a pronunciation guide in italics. Read it as if it were English and you should be understood, but remember that it is only a guide and for the best results you should listen to the native speakers in the audio app and try to mimic them. Some French sounds are different from those in English, so take note of how the letters below are pronounced.

a, à, â	like "a" in "father"
au	like "o" in "over"
c	before "a", "o", and "u", like "k" in "kite" before "e" and "i", like "s" in "sun"
ç	like "s" in "sun"
cc	like "cc" in "accident"
ch	like "sh" in "ship"
e, eu	like "u" in "puff"
è, ê, e	like "e" in "fetch"
e, ez, er	like "ay" in "play"
g	before "a," "o," and "u," like "g" in "get" before "e," "i," and "y," like "s" in "leisure"
h	silent
i	like "ee" in "feet"
j	like "s" in "leisure"
o	like "o" in "toll"
oi	like "wa" in "wag"
ou	like "oo" in "shoot"
qu	like "k" in "kite"
r	rolled at the back of the throat
u	like "ew" in "dew"
ui	like "wee" in "between"
w	like "v" in "van"

FREE EYEWITNESS TRAVEL PHRASE BOOK AUDIO APP

The audio app that accompanies this phrase book contains nearly 1,000 essential French words and phrases, spoken by native speakers, for use when traveling or when preparing for your trip.

HOW TO USE THE AUDIO APP

- Download the free app on your smartphone or tablet from the App Store or Google Play.
- Open the app and scan or key in the barcode on the back of your Eyewitness Phrase Book to add the book to your Library.
- Download the audio files for your language.
- The 🎧 symbol in the book indicates that there is audio for that section. Enter the page number from the book into the search field in the app to bring up the list of words and phrases for that page or section. You can then scroll up and down through the list to find the word or phrase you want.
- Tap a word or phrase to hear it.
- Swipe left or right to view the previous or next page.
- Add phrases you will use often to your Favorites.

ESSENTIALS

In this section, you will find the essential words and useful phrases you need for basic everyday situations and for getting to know people. Be aware of cultural differences when you are addressing French people, and remember that they tend to be quite formal when greeting each other, using *Monsieur* for men, *Madame* for women and *Mademoiselle* for girls and younger women, and often shaking hands.

GREETINGS

Hello	Bonjour *bohnjoor*
Good evening	Bonsoir *bohnswar*
Good night	Bonne nuit *bonn nwee*
Goodbye	Au revoir *oh ruhvwar*
Hi/bye!	Salut! *sahlew*
How are you?	Comment ça va? *komohn sah vah*
Fine, thanks	Bien, merci *byahn mairsee*
You're welcome	De rien *duh ryahn*
My name is...	Je m'appelle... *juh mahpel*
What's your name?	Vous vous appelez comment? *voo voo zahpuhlay komohn*
What's his/her name?	Comment s'appelle-t-il/elle? *komohn sahpel teel/tel*
This is...	C'est... *say*
Pleased to meet you	Enchanté/Enchantée *ohnshohntay*
See you tomorrow	À demain *ah duhmahn*
See you soon	À bientôt *ah byahntoh*

SMALL TALK

Yes/No	Oui/Non *wee/nohn*
Please	S'il vous plaît *seel voo play*
Thank you (very much)	Merci (beaucoup) *mairsee (bohkoo)*
You're welcome	De rien *duh ryahn*
OK/Fine	D'accord/Bien *dahkohr/byahn*
Pardon?	Pardon? *pardohn*
Excuse me	Excusez-moi *exkewzay mwa*
Sorry	Désolé/Désolée *dayzolay*
I don't know	Je ne sais pas *juh nuh say pah*
I don't understand	Je ne comprends pas *juh nuh kohnprohn pah*
Could you repeat that?	Vous pouvez répéter? *voo poovay raypaytay*
I don't speak French	Je ne parle pas français *juh nuh parl pah frohnsay*
Do you speak English?	Vous parlez anglais? *voo parlay ohnglay*
What is the French for...?	Comment dit-on...en français? *komohn dee tohn...ohn frohnsay*
What's that called?	Ça s'appelle comment? *sah sahpel komohn*
Can you tell me...	Vous pouvez me dire... *voo poovay muh deer*

TALKING ABOUT YOURSELF

I'm from...	Je viens de... *juh vyahn duh*
I'm...	Je suis... *juh swee*
...American	...américain/américaine *ahmaireekahn/ahmaireeken*
...English	...anglais/anglaise *ohnglay/ohnglaiz*
...Canadian	...canadien/canadienne *kanadyahn/kanadyen*
...Australian	...australien/australienne *ohstrahlyahn/ohstrahlyen*
...single	...célibataire *sayleebahtair*
...married	...marié/mariée *maryay*
...divorced	...divorcé/divorcée *deevohrsay*
I am...years old	J'ai...ans *jay...ohn*
I have...	J'ai... *jay*
...a boyfriend/girlfriend	...un copain/une copine *uhn kohpahn/ewn kohpeen*
...two children	...deux enfants *duh zohnfohn*
Where are you from?	Vous êtes d'où? *voo zayt doo*
Are you married?	Vous êtes marié/mariée? *voo zayt maryay*
Do you have children?	Vous avez des enfants? *voo zavay day zohnfohn*

SOCIALIZING

Do you live here?	Vous habitez ici? *voo zahbeetay eesee*
Where do you live?	Vous habitez où? *voo zahbeetay oo*
I am here...	Je suis ici... *juh swee eesee*
...on vacation	...en vacances *ohn vahkohns*
...on business	...pour affaires *poor ahfair*
I'm a student	Je suis étudiant/étudiante *juh swee aytewdyohn/aytewdyohnt*
I work in...	Je travaille dans... *juh trahvaeey dohn*
I am retired	Je suis retraité/retraitée *juh swee ruhtraytay*
Can I have...	Je peux avoir... *juh puh avwar*
...your telephone number?	...votre numéro de téléphone? *vohtr newmairo duh taylayfon*
...your email address?	...votre adresse e-mail? *vohtr ahdress e-mail*
It doesn't matter	Ce n'est pas grave *suh nay pah grahv*
Cheers!	Santé! *sohntay*
Are you alright?	Ça va? *sah vah*
I'm OK	Ça va *sah vah*
What do you think?	Qu'est-ce que vous en pensez ? *kes kuh voo zohn pohnsay*

LIKES AND DISLIKES

I like/love...   J'aime/j'adore...
jaym/jahdohr

I don't like...   Je n'aime pas...
juh naym pah

I hate...   Je déteste...
juh daytest

I rather/really like...   J'aime bien/j'aime beaucoup...
jaym byahn/jaym bohkoo

Do you like...?   Vous aimez...?
voo zaymay

Don't you like it?   Vous n'aimez pas ça?
voo naymay pah sah

I would like...   J'aimerais...
jaymuhray

I'd like this one/that one   Je voudrais celui-ci/celui-là
juh voodray suhlwee see/suhlwee lah

My favorite is...   Mon préféré, c'est...
mohn prayfayray say

I prefer...   Je préfère...
juh prayfayr

It's delicious   C'est délicieux
say dayleesyuh

What would you like to do?   Qu'est-ce que vous voulez faire?
kes kuh voo voolay fair

I don't mind   Ça m'est égal
sah may taygahl

YOU MAY HEAR...

Vous faites quoi dans la vie?
voo fet kwa dohn lah vee
What do you do?

Vous êtes en vacances?
voo zayt ohn vahkohns
Are you on vacation?

DAYS OF THE WEEK

Sunday	dimanche *deemohnsh*	**Saturday**	samedi *samdee*
Monday	lundi *luhndee*	**today**	aujourd'hui *ohjoordwee*
Tuesday	mardi *mardee*	**tomorrow**	demain *duhmahn*
Wednesday	mercredi *maircruhdee*	**yesterday**	hier *eeyair*
Thursday	jeudi *juhdee*	**in...days**	dans...jours *dohn...joor*
Friday	vendredi *vohndruhdee*	**What day is it today?**	Quel jour sommes-nous aujourd'hui? *kel joor sohm noo ohjoordwee*

THE SEASONS

le printemps
luh prahntohn
spring

l'été
laytay
summer

MONTHS

January	janvier *johnvyay*	July	juillet *jweeyay*
February	février *fayvreeyay*	August	août *oot*
March	mars *mars*	September	septembre *sayptohnbr*
April	avril *ahvreel*	October	octobre *ohktohbr*
May	mai *may*	November	novembre *nohvohnbr*
June	juin *jwahn*	December	décembre *daysohnbr*

l'automne
lohtonn
fall

l'hiver
leevair
winter

TELLING THE TIME

What time is it?	Quelle heure est-il? *kel uhr ay teel*
It's nine o'clock	Il est neuf heures *eel ay nuhvuhr*
...in the morning	...du matin *dew mahtahn*
...in the afternoon	...de l'après-midi *duh lahpray meedee*
...in the evening	...du soir *dew swar*

une heure
ewn uhr
one o'clock

une heure dix
ewn uhr dees
ten past one

une heure et quart
ewn uhr ay kar
quarter past one

une heure vingt
ewn uhr vahn
twenty past one

une heure et demie
ewn uhr ay duhmee
half past one

deux heures
moins le quart
*duh zuhr mwahn
luh kar*
quarter to two

deux heures
moins dix
*duh zuhr
mwahn dees*
ten to two

deux heures
duhzuhr
two o'clock

It's noon/midnight	Il est midi/minuit *eel ay meedee/meenwee*
second	la seconde *lah suhgohnd*
minute	la minute *lah meenewt*
hour	l'heure *luhr*
a quarter of an hour	un quart d'heure *uhn kar duhr*
half an hour	une demi-heure *ewn duhmee uhr*
three-quarters of an hour	trois quarts d'heure *trwa kar duhr*
late	tard *tar*
early	tôt *toh*
soon	bientôt *byahntoh*
What time does it start?	À quelle heure ça commence? *ah kel uhr sah komohns*
What time does it finish?	À quelle heure ça finit? *ah kel uhr sah feenee*

YOU MAY HEAR...

À plus tard *ah plew tar* **See you later**	Vous êtes en avance *voo zayt ohn nahvohns* **You're early**	Vous êtes en retard *voo zayt ohn ruhtar* **You're late**

THE WEATHER

What's the weather like?	Quel temps fait-il? *kel tohn fayteel*
It's...	Il fait... *eel fay*
...good	...beau *boh*
...bad	...mauvais *mohvay*
...warm	...bon *bohn*
...hot	...chaud *shoh*
...cold	...froid *frwa*
...humid	...humide *ewmeed*

Il y a du soleil
*eeleeya
dew sohlay*
It's sunny

Il pleut
eel pluh
It's raining

Il y a des
nuages
*eeleeya day
newahj*
It's cloudy

Il y a une
tempête
*eeleeya
ewn tohnpet*
It's stormy

What's the forecast?	Quelles sont les prévisions météo? *kel sohn lay prayveezyohn maytayoh*
What's the temperature?	Quelle température fait-il? *kel tohnpayrahtewr fayteel*
It's...degrees	Il fait...degrés *eel fay…duhgray*
It's a beautiful day	C'est une belle journée *say tewn bel joornay*
The weather's changing	Le temps change *luh tohn shohnj*
Is it going to get colder/ hotter?	Il va faire plus froid/chaud? *eel vah fair plew frwa/shoh*
It's cooling down	Le temps se rafraîchit *luh tohn suh rahfrayshee*
Is it going to freeze?	Il va geler? *eel vah juhlay*

Il neige
eel nayj
It's snowing

Il gèle
eel jayl
It's icy

Il y a du
brouillard
*eeleeya dew
brooyar*
It's misty

Il y a du
vent
*eeleeya
dew vohn*
It's windy

GETTING AROUND

France has an excellent road and freeway system
if you are traveling around the country by car. French
trains are fast and punctual, linking the main towns
and cities, while in the countryside buses connect most
mainline train stations with towns and villages not
served by trains. You can also travel by taxi, tram,
plane or, in some cities, the *Métro* (subway).

ASKING WHERE THINGS ARE

Excuse me, please	Excusez-moi, s'il vous plaît *exkewzay mwa seel voo play*
Where is...	Où se trouve... *oo suh troov*
...the town center?	...le centre-ville? *luh sohntruh veel*
...the train station?	...la gare? *lah gar*
...the cash machine?	...le distributeur? *luh deestreebewtuhr*
How do I get to...?	Pour aller à...? *poor allay ah*
I'm going to...	Je vaisà... *juh vayah*
I'm looking for...	Je cherche... *juh shayrsh*
I'm lost	Je suis perdu/perdue *juh swee payrdew*
Is it near?	C'est près d'ici? *say pray deesee*
Is there a...nearby?	Y a-t-il un...près d'ici? *yateel uhn...pray deesee*
Is it far?	C'est loin? *say lwahn*
How far is...	À quelle distance se trouve... *a kel deestohns suh troov*
...the town hall?	...la mairie? *lah mairee*
...the market?	...le marché? *luh marshay*
Can I walk there?	On peut y aller à pied? *ohn puh ee allay ah peeyayvwatewr*

CAR AND BIKE RENTAL

Where is the car rental desk?	Où se trouve l'agence de location de voitures? *oo suh troov lajohns duh lokahsyohn duh vwatewr*
I want to rent...	Je voudrais louer... *juh voodray looay*
...a car	...une voiture *ewn vwatewr*
...a motorcycle	...une moto *ewn moto*
...a bicycle	...un vélo *uhn vaylo*
for...days	pour...jours *poor...joor*

la berline
lah bairleen
sedan

le coupé
luh coopay
hatchback

la moto
lah moto
motorcycle

le scooter
luh scooter
scooter

le VTT
luh vaytaytay
mountain bike

le vélo de ville
luh vaylo duh veel
road bike

for the weekend	pour le week-end *poor luh weekend*
I'd like...	Je voudrais... *juh voodray*
...an automatic	...une automatique *ewn automateek*
...a manual	...une manuelle *ewn manewayl*
Has it got air-conditioning?	Il y a la climatisation? *eeleeya lah cleemateezasyohn*
Should I return it with a full tank?	Je dois la rendre avec le plein d'essence? *juh dwa lah rohndr avek luh plahn daysohns*
Here's my driver's license	Voici mon permis *vwassee mohn pairmee*
Can I rent a GPS receiver...?	Je peux louer un...GPS? *juh puh looay uhn jaypayes*
Do you have a...	Vous avez... *voozavay*

un casque de vélo
uhn kask duh vaylo
cycling helmet

une pompe
ewn pohnp
pump

un antivol
uhn ohnteevol
lock

un siège enfant
uhn siayj ohnfohn
child seat

DRIVING

Is this the road to...?	Cette route mène-t-elle à...?
	set root mayn tayl ah
Where is...	Où se trouve...
	oo suh troov
...the nearest garage?	...le garage le plus proche?
	luh garaj luh plew prosh
I'd like...	Je voudrais...
	juh voodray
...some gas	...de l'essence
	duh laysohns
...40 liters of unleaded	...40 litres de sans plomb
	kahrohnt leetruh duh sohn plohn
...30 liters of diesel	...30 litres de diésel
	trohnt leetruh duh dyayzayl
Fill it up, please	Le plein, s'il vous plaît
	luh plahn, seel voo play
Where do I pay?	Je paye où?
	juh payuh oo
The pump number is...	Le numéro de la pompe est le...
	luh newmairo duh lah pohnp ay luh
Can I pay by credit card?	Je peux payer par carte bancaire?
	juh puh payay par cart bohnkair
Please can you check...	Vous pouvez vérifier...
	voo poovay vayreefyay
...the oil	...le niveau d'huile
	luh neevoh dweel
...the tire pressure	...la pression des pneus
	lah praysyon day pnuh

PARKING

Is there a parking lot nearby?	Y a-t-il un parking près d'ici? *yateel uhn parking pray deesee*
Can I park here?	Je peux me garer ici? *juh puh muh garay eesee*
Is it free?	C'est gratuit? *say gratwee*
How much does it cost?	Ça coûte combien? *sa koot kombyahn*
How much is it...	C'est combien... *say kombyahn*
...per hour?	...par heure? *par uhr*
...per day?	...par jour? *par joor*
...overnight?	....pour une nuit? *poor ewn nwee*

la galerie
lah galree
roofrack

le siège enfant
luh siayj ohnfohn
child seat

la station-service
lah stahsyohn sairvees
gas station

THE CAR

le coffre
luh kohfruh
trunk

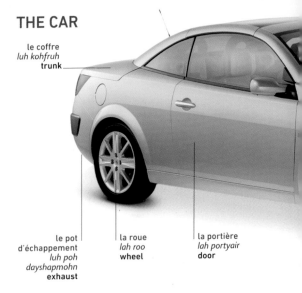

le pot
d'échappement
*luh poh
dayshapmohn*
exhaust

la roue
lah roo
wheel

la portière
lah portyair
door

INSIDE THE CAR

l'appuie-tête
lapwee tayt
head rest

la poignée
lah pwanyay
handle

le siège avant
luh siayj avohn
front seat

la serrure
lah sairewr
door lock

la ceinture
de sécurité
*lah sahntewr duh
saykewreetay*
seat belt

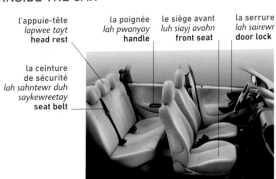

le pare-brise
luh par breez
windshield

le capot
luh kapo
hood

le phare
luh far
headlight

le pneu
luh pnuh
tire

le moteur
luh motuhr
engine

le pare-choc
luh par shok
bumper

THE CONTROLS

la radio
lah rahdyoh
car stereo

les feux de détresse
lay fuh duh daytrays
hazard lights

le compteur
de vitesse
*luh kohntuhr
duh veetess*
speedometer

l'airbag
lairbag
airbag

le chauffage
luh shofaj
heater

le levier de
vitesses
*luh luhvyay
duh veetess*
gear shift

le tableau de
bord
*luh tabloh
duh bohr*
dashboard

le klaxon
luh klaxon
horn

le volant
luh volohn
steering wheel

ROAD SIGNS

sens unique
sohns ewneek
one way

rond-point
rohn pwuhn
traffic circle

cédez le passage
sayday luh passaj
yield

route prioritaire
root preeyoreetair
priority road

sens interdit
sohns ihntairdee
no entry

défense de stationner
dayfohns duh stasyonay
no parking

défense de s'arrêter
dayfohns duh saraytay
no stopping

limitation de vitesse
leemeetasyohn duh veetess
speed limit

danger
dohnjay
hazard

ON THE ROAD

l'horodateur
lohrodatuhr
parking meter

les feux
lay fuh
traffic lights

l'agent de la circulation
lajohn duh lah seerkewlasyohn
traffic police officer

le passage piéton
luh pasaj pyaytohn
pedestrian crossing

la carte
lah kart
map

la place de parking
réservée aux handicapés
*lah plas duh parking
rayzairvay ozohndeekapay*
disabled parking

l'autoroute
lotoroot
highway

la voie d'accès
lah vwa daksay
entrance/exit ramp

le téléphone d'urgence
luh taylayfon dewrjohns
emergency phone

AT THE STATION

Where can I buy a ticket?	Où peut-on acheter des billets? *oo puh tohn ashuhtay day beeyay*
Is there an automatic ticket machine?	Y a-t-il un guichet automatique? *yateel uhn geeshay automateek*
How much is a ticket to...?	Combien coûte un billet pour...? *kombyahn koot uhn beeyay poor*
Do I stamp the ticket before boarding?	Il faut composter avant de prendre le train? *eel fo kohnpostay ahvohn duh prohndruh luh trahn*
Two tickets to...	Deux billets pour... *duh beeyay poor*
I'd like...	Je voudrais... *juh voodray*
...a onw-way ticket to...	...un aller simple pour... *uhn allay sahnpl poor*
...a return ticket to...	...un aller-retour pour... *uhn allay ruhtoor poor*
...a first-class ticket	...un billet première classe *uhn beeyay pruhmyair class*
...a standard-class ticket	...un billet deuxième classe *uhn beeyay duhzyaym class*

le guichet automatique
luh geeshay automateek
automatic ticket machine

le billet
luh beeyay
ticket

I'd like to...	Je voudrais... *juh voodray*
...reserve a seat	...réserver une place *rayzairvay ewn plass*
...book a sleeper berth	...réserver une couchette *rayzairvay ewn kooshet*
...on the TGV to...	...dans le TGV pour... *dohn luh tayjayvay poor*
Is there a reduction...?	Il y a une réduction...? *eeleeya ewn raydewksyohn*
...for children?	...pour les enfants? *poor layzohnfohn*
...for students?	...pour les étudiants? *poor layzaytewdyohn*
...for senior citizens?	...pour les personnes âgées? *poor lay pairson zahjay*
Is there a dining car?	Il y a un wagon-restaurant? *eeleeya uhn vahgon raystohrohn*
Is it a fast/slow train?	C'est un train rapide/omnibus? *say uhn trahn rapeed/omnibews*
Is it a high-speed train?	C'est un train à grande vitesse? *say uhn trahn ah grand veetess*

YOU MAY HEAR...

Le train partira de la voie...
luh trahn parteera duh lah vwa
The train leaves from platform...

Il faut changer de train
eel fo shohnjay duh trahn
You must change trains

TRAVELING BY TRAIN

Do you have a timetable?
Vous avez les horaires?
voozavay layzorair

What time is...
À quelle heure est...
ah kel uhr ay

...the next train to...?
... le prochain train pour...?
luh proshahn trahn poor

...the last train to...?
... le dernier train pour...?
luh dairnyay trahn poor

Which platform does it leave from?
De quelle voie part-il?
duh kel vwa parteel

What time does it arrive in...?
À quelle heure arrive-t-il à...?
akel uhr areevteel ah

How long does it take?
Combien de temps dure le voyage?
kombyahn duh tohn dewr luh vwayaj

Is this the train for...?
C'est le train pour...?
say luh trahn poor

Is this the right platform for...?
C'est le bon quai pour...?
say luh bohn kay poor

Where is platform three?
Le quai numéro trois, s'il vous plaît?
luh kay newmairo trwa, seel voo play

Does this train stop at...?
Ce train s'arrête à...?
suh trahn sarayt ah

YOU MAY HEAR...

Il faut composter son billet
eel foh kohnpostay sohn beeyay
You must validate your ticket

Utilisez la borne orange
ewteeleezay lah born orohnj
Use the orange machine

Where do I change for...?

Je dois changer où pour...?
juh dwa shohnjay oo poor

Is this seat free?

Cette place est libre?
set plass eh libruh

I've reserved this seat

J'ai une réservation pour cette place
jay ewn rayzairvasyohn poor set plass

Do I get off here?

Je descends ici?
juh daysohn eesee

Where is the subway station?

Où se trouve la station de métro?
oo suh troov lah stahsyohn duh maytroh

Which line goes to...?

Quelle est la ligne pour...?
kel ay lah leenyuh poor

How many stops is it?

C'est dans combien d'arrêts?
say dohn kombyahn daray

le hall de gare
luh ohl duh gar
concourse

le train
luh trahn
train

le wagon-
restaurant
*luh vagohn
raystohrohn*
dining car

la couchette
lah kooshet
sleeper berth

BUSES

When is the next bus to...?
À quelle heure est le prochain bus pour...?
ah kel uhr ay luh proshahn bews poor

What is the fare to...?
Combien coûte le ticket pour...?
kombyahn koot luh teekay poor

Where is the bus stop?
Où se trouve l'arrêt de bus?
oo suh troov laray duh bews

Is this the bus stop for...
C'est l'arrêt pour...
say laray poor

Does the number 4 stop here?
Le quatre s'arrête ici?
luh katr sarayt eesee

Where can I buy a ticket?
Où peut-on acheter des tickets?
oo puh tohn ashuhtay day teekay

Can I pay on the bus?
Je peux payer dans le bus?
juh puh payay dohn luh bews

Which buses go to the city center?
Quels bus vont au centre ville?
kel bews vohnt oh sohntruh veel

Will you tell me when to get off?
Vous m'indiquerez quand descendre?
voo mahndeekeray kohn daysohndruh

I want to get off!
Je veux descendre!
juh vuh daysohndruh

le bus
luh bews
bus

la gare routière
lah gar rootyair
bus station

TAXIS

Where can I get a taxi?	Où peut-on trouver un taxi? *oo puh tohn troovay uhn taxi*
Can I order a taxi?	Je peux commander un taxi? *juh puh komohnday uhn taxi*
I want a taxi to...	Je voudrais un taxi pour aller à... *juh voodray uhn taxi poor allay ah*
Can you take me to...	Pouvez-vous m'emmener à... *poovay voo mohnmuhnay ah*
Is it far?	C'est loin? *say lwahn*
How much will it cost?	Quel sera le prix de la course? *kel suhrah luh pree duh la koors*
Can you drop me here?	Vous pouvez me laisser là? *voo poovay muh laysay la*
What do I owe you?	Je vous dois combien? *juh voo dwa kombyahn*
Keep the change	Gardez la monnaie *garday lah monay*
May I have a receipt?	Je peux avoir un reçu? *juh puh avwar uhn ruhsew*
Please wait for me	Attendez-moi *atohnday mwa*

le taxi
luh taxi
taxi

la station de taxis
lah stasyohn duh taxi
taxi stand

BOATS

Are there any boat trips?	Y a-t-il des balades en bateau? *eeyateel day balad ohn bato*
Where does the boat leave from?	D'où part le bateau? *doo par luh bato*
When is...	À quelle heure part... *a kel uhr par*
...the next boat to...?	...le prochain bateau pour... *luh proshahn bato poor*
...the first boat?	... le premier bateau? *luh pruhmyay bato*
...the last boat?	... le dernier bateau? *luh dairnyay bato*
I'd like two tickets for...	Je voudrais deux billets pour *juh voodray duh beeyay poor*
...the cruise	...la croisière *lah krwazyair*
...the river trip	...la balade en rivière *lah balad ohn reevyair*

le ferry
luh ferry
ferry

l'hydroglisseur
leedrogleessuhr
hydrofoil

le yacht
luh yaht
yacht

l'aéroglisseur
lahairogleessuhr
hovercraft

How much is it for...	C'est combien pour... *say kombyahn poor*
...a car?	...une voiture? *ewn vwatewr*
...a family?	...une famille? *ewn fameey*
...a cabin?	...une cabine? *ewn kahbeen*
Can I buy a ticket on board?	On peut acheter les billets une fois sur le bateau? *ohn puh ashuhtay leh beeyay ewn fwa sewr luh bato*
Is there wheelchair access?	Il y a un accès handicapés? *eeleeya uhn aksay ohndeekapay*

le bateau de plaisance
luh bato duh playzohns
pleasure boat

la bouée de sauvetage
lah booay duh sovtaj
life ring

le catamaran
luh catamarohn
catamaran

le gilet de sauvetage
luh jeelay duh sovtaj
life jacket

AIR TRAVEL

Which terminal do I need?	Je vais à quel terminal?
	juh vay ah kel tairmeenal
Where do I check in?	Où se trouve l'enregistrement?
	oo suh troov lohnruhjeestruhmohn
Where is/are...	Où se trouve/trouvent...
	oo suh troov
...the arrivals hall?	...les arrivées?
	lay zareevay
...the departures hall?	...les départs?
	lay daypar
...the boarding gate?	...l'embarquement?
	lohnbarkuhmohn
I'm traveling...	Je voyage...
	juh vwayaj
...economy	...en classe économique
	ohn class aykonomik
...business class	...en classe affaires
	ohn class ahfair
Here is my...	Voici mon/ma...
	vwassee mohn/mah

le sac fourre-tout
luh sac foor too
duffel bag

le passeport
luh passpor
passport

le repas
servi à bord
*luh ruhpah
sairvee ah bohr*
in-flight meal

la carte
d'embarquement
*lah kart
dohnbarkuhmohn*
boarding pass

I'm checking in one suitcase	J'ai une valise à enregistrer *jay ewn valeez ah ohnruhjeestray*
I packed it myself	J'ai fait mes bagages moi-même *jay fay may bagaj mwa maym*
I have one piece of hand luggage	J'ai un bagage à main *jay uhn bagaj ah mahn*
What is the weight allowance?	Quel est le poids maximum autorisé? *kel ay luh pwa mahkseemuhm ohtohreezay*
How much is excess baggage?	Combien coûte l'excédent de bagages? *kombyahn koot layksaydohn duh bagaj*
Will a meal be served?	Un repas est servi dans l'avion? *uhn ruhpah ay sairvee dohn lahvyohn*
I'd like...	Je voudrais... *juh voodray*
...a window seat	...une place fenêtre *ewn plass fuhnaytr*
...an aisle seat	...une place couloir *ewn plass koolwar*

YOU MAY HEAR...

Votre passeport/billet, s'il vous plaît
votruh passpor/beeyay seel voo play
Your passport/ticket, please

C'est votre sac?
say votruh sack
Is this your bag?

AT THE AIRPORT

Here's my...	Voici... *vwassee*
...boarding pass	...ma carte d'embarquement *ma kart dohnbarkuhmohn*
...passport	...mon passeport *mohn passpor*
Can I change some money?	Je peux faire du change? *juh puh fair dew shohnj*
What is the exchange rate?	Quel est le taux de change? *kel ay luh toduh shohnj*
Is the flight to...on time?	Le vol pour...est à l'heure? *luh vol poor...ayt a luhr*
Is the flight delayed?	Le vol a du retard? *luh vol a dew ruhtar*

l'enregistrement
lohnruhjeestruhmohn
check-in

le bureau de change
luh bewro duh shohj
**currency exchange
booth**

le contrôle des
passeports
luh kohntrol day passpor
passport control

le magasin hors taxe
luh magazahn or tax
duty-free shop

le retrait des bagages
luh ruhtray day bagaj
baggage claim

le pilote
luh peelot
pilot

l'avion
lavyohn
airplane

l'hôtesse de l'air
lotess duh lair
flight attendant

How late is it?	Il a combien de retard? *eeleeya kombyahn duh ruhtar*
Which gate does flight... leave from?	Le vol numéro...part de quelle porte d'embarquement? *luh vol newmairo...par duh kel portuh dohnbarkuhmohn*
What time do I board?	À quelle heure est l'embarquement? *a kel uhr ay lohnbarkuhmohn*
Where are the carts?	Où sont les chariots? *oo sohn lay shareeo*
I can't find my baggage	Je ne trouve pas mes bagages *juh nuh troov pa may bagaj*

EATING OUT

It is not difficult to eat well and inexpensively in France. You can choose from cafés and bars, which serve a variety of drinks and snacks, *bistros* (small bars which are often family-run and serve local and traditional dishes) and *brasseries*, which are usually larger and noisier. If you want a gastronomic meal in more formal surroundings, you can eat at a more expensive restaurant but you may have to book in advance.

MAKING A RESERVATION

I'd like to book a table...	Je voudrais réserver une table... *juh voodray rayzairvay ewn tabluh*
...for lunch/dinner	...pour déjeuner/dîner *poor dayjuhnay/deenay*
...for four people	...pour quatre personnes *poor katruh pairson*
...for this evening at seven	...pour ce soir à sept heures *poor suh swar a set uhr*
...for tomorrow at one	...pour demain à une heure *poor duhmahn a ewn uhr*
...for lunchtime today	...pour déjeuner, aujourd'hui *poor dayjuhnay ohjoordwee*
Do you have a table earlier/later?	Vous avez une table un peu plus tôt/tard? *voo zavay ewn tabluh uhn puh plew toh/tar*
My name is...	Je m'appelle... *juh mapel*
My telephone number is...	Mon numéro de téléphone est le... *mohn newmairo duh taylayfon ay luh*
I have a reservation	J'ai réservé *jay rayzairvay*
in the name of...	au nom de... *o nohn duh*
We haven't booked	Nous n'avons pas réservé *noo navohn pa rayzairvay*
May we sit here?	On peut s'asseoir ici? *ohn puh sasswar eesee*
May we sit outside?	On peut s'asseoir dehors? *ohn puh sasswar duhor*
I'm waiting for someone	J'attends quelqu'un *jatohn kaylkuhn*

ORDERING A MEAL

May we see the menu	La carte, s'il vous plaît *lah kart seel voo play*
...the wine list	La carte des vins, s'il vous plaît *lah kart day vahn seel voo play*
Do you have...	Vous avez... *voo zavay*
...a set menu?	...un menu? *uhn muhnew*
...a fixed-price menu?	...un menu du jour? *uhn muhnew dew joor*
...a children's menu?	...un menu pour enfants? *uhn muhnew poor ohnfohn*
...an à la carte menu?	...une carte? *ewn kart*
What are today's specials?	Il y a des plats du jour? *eeleeya day plah dew joor*
What do you recommend?	Qu'est-ce-que vous recommandez? *kes kuh voo ruhkomohnday*
What is this?	Qu'est-ce que c'est? *kes kuh say*

YOU MAY HEAR...

Vous avez réservé?
voo zavay rayzairvay
Do you have a reservation?

Asseyez-vous
ahsayay voo
Please be seated

À quel nom?
ah kel nohn
In what name?

Vous avez choisi?
voo zavay shwazee
Are you ready to order?

Are there any vegetarian dishes?	Vous avez des plats végétariens? *voo zavay deh plah vayjaytahryahn*
I can't eat...	Je suis allergique... *juh sweez ahlairjeek*
...dairy foods	...aux produits laitiers *oh prohdwee laytyay*
...nuts	...aux noix *oh nwa*
...wheat	...au blé *oh blay*
To start, I'll have...	En entrée, je vais prendre... *ohn ohntray juh vay prohndr*
May we have...	On peut avoir... *ohn puh avwar*
...some water	...de l'eau? *duh loh*
...some bread?	...du pain? *dew pahn*
...the dessert menu?	...la carte des desserts? *lah kart day dayssair*

READING THE MENU...

entrées/hors-d'œuvre *ohntray/ohr duhvr* **appetizers**	légumes *laygewm* **vegetables**	desserts *dayssair* **desserts**
plats principaux *plah prahnseepoh* **main courses**	fromages *frohmaj* **cheeses**	

COMPLAINING

I didn't order this	Je n'ai pas commandé ça *juh nay pah komohnday sa*
You forgot my dessert	Vous avez oublié mon dessert *voozavay oobleeay mohn dayssair*
I can't wait any longer	Je ne peux plus attendre *juh nuh puh plews atohndru*

PAYING

That was delicious	C'était délicieux *saytay dayleessyuh*
The check, please	L'addition, s'il vous plaît *ladeesyohn seel voo play*
May I have...	Je peux avoir... *juh puh avwar*
...a receipt?	...un reçu? *uhn ruhssew*
...an itemized bill?	...une addition détaillée? *lewn adeesyohn daytaeey*
Is service included?	Le service est compris? *luh sairvees ay kohnpree*
There's a mistake here	Il y a une erreur ici *eeleeyah ewn airuhr eesee*

DISHES AND CUTLERY

la petite assiette
lah puhteet assyet
side plate

le bol
luh bohl
bowl

le sel
luh sayl
salt

le poivre
luh pwahvruh
pepper

la cuiller à dessert
lah kweeyair ah dayssair
dessert spoon

la tasse et la soucoupe
lah tass ay lah sookoop
cup and saucer

le verre
luh vair
glass

la cuiller à café
la kweeyair ah kafay
teaspoon

la fourchette
lah foorshet
fork

le couteau
luh kooto
knife

l'assiette
lassyet
dinner plate

la serviette
lah sairvyet
napkin

AT THE CAFÉ OR BAR

The menu, please	Le menu, s'il vous plaît *luh muhnew seel voo play*
Do you have...?	Vous avez...? *voozavay*
What fruit juices do you have?	Quels jus de fruits avez-vous? *kel jew duh frwee avayvoo*
I'd like...	Je voudrais... *juh voodray*
I'll have...	Je vais prendre... *juh vay prohndruh*

un café au lait
uhn kafay o lay
coffee with milk

un café noir
uhn kafay nwar
black coffee

un expresso
uhn expresso
espresso

un cappuccino
uhn kapoocheeno
cappuccino

YOU MAY HEAR...

Vous désirez?
voo dayzeeray
What would you like?

Autre chose?
otruh shoz
Anything else?

Ça sera tout?
sa suhra too
Will that be all?

un thé au lait/thé nature
uhn tay o lay/tay natewr
tea with milk/black tea

un thé au citron
uhn tay o seetrohn
tea with lemon

un thé à la menthe
uhn tay a lah mohnt
mint tea

un thé vert
uhn tay vair
green tea

une camomille
ewn kamomeey
chamomile tea

un chocolat chaud
uhn shokolah sho
hot chocolate

A bottle of...	Une bouteille de... *ewn bootayeey duh*
A glass of...	Un verre de... *uhn vair duh*
A cup of...	Une tasse de... *ewn tass duh*
With lemon/milk	Avec du citron/du lait *avek dew seetrohn/dew lay*
Another...please	Un/une autre...s'il vous plaît *uhn/ewn otruh seel voo play*
The same again, please	La même chose, s'il vous plaît *la maym shoz seel voo play*

CAFÉ AND BAR DRINKS

un jus d'ananas
uhn jew danana
pineapple juice

un jus de pomme
uhn jew duh pom
apple juice

un jus d'orange
uhn jew dorohnj
orange juice

une limonade
ewn leemonahd
lemonade

un jus de raisin
uhn jew duh rayzahn
grape juice

un jus de tomate
uhn jew duh tomaht
tomato juice

un gin tonic
uhn djeen tonic
gin and tonic

un coca
unh kokah
cola

un café frappé
uhn kafay frapay
iced coffee

une orangeade
ewn orohnjad
orangeade

une eau pétillante
ewn o payteeyohnt
soda water

une bière
ewn byair
beer

une bouteille d'eau minérale
ewn bootayeey do meenairal
bottle of mineral water

un cidre
uhn seedruh
cider

du vin blanc
dew vahn blohn
white wine

un verre de vin rouge
uhn vair duh vahn rooj
glass of red wine

YOU MAY HEAR...

Un demi?   En bouteille?
uhn duhmee *ohn bootayee*
A half?   **Bottled?**

Plate ou pétillante?
plaht oo payteeyohnt
Still or sparkling?

Avec des glaçons?
avek day glassohn
With ice?

BAR SNACKS

un sandwich
uhn sohndweech
sandwich

un croque-monsieur
uhn krok-muhsyuh
**grilled cheese and
ham sandwich**

des olives
day zoleev
olives

des cacahouètes
day kakaooet
peanuts

de la vinaigrette
duh lah veenaygret
dressing

une salade
ewn salad
salad

des galettes
day galet
**savory
crêpes**

une viennoiserie
ewn vyaynwazuhree
pastry

une glace
ewn glass
ice cream

de la brioche
duh lah breeosh
brioche

FAST FOOD

May I have...
Je voudrais...
juh voodray

...to eat in/carry out
...sur place/à emporter
sewr plass/ah ohnportay

...some ketchup/mustard
...du ketchup/de la moutarde
dew ketchup/duh lah mootard

un hamburger
uhn ohnbuhrguhr
hamburger

un hamburger
au poulet
*uhn ohnbuhrguhr
oh poolay*
chicken burger

un wrap
uhn rap
wrap

un hot-dog
uhn ot dog
hot dog

des brochettes
day broshet
kebabs

des frites
day freet
French fries

du poulet frit
dew poolay free
fried chicken

une pizza
ewn pizza
pizza

BREAKFAST

May I have some...	Je peux avoir... *juh puh avwar*
...milk/sugar	...du lait/du sucre *dew lay/dew sewkr*
...artificial sweetener	...de l'édulcorant *duh laydewlkorohn*
...butter	...du beurre *dew buhr*

un café
uhn kafay
coffee

un thé
uhn tay
tea

un chocolat
chaud
uhn shokolah sho
hot chocolate

un jus d'orange
uhn jew dorohnj
orange juice

un jus de pomme
uhn jew duh pom
apple juice

du pain
dew pahn
bread

du pain perdu
dew pahn pairdew
French toast

de la brioche
duh lah breeosh
brioche

un petit pain
uhn puhtee pahn
bread roll

un croissant
uhn krwassohn
croissant

un pain au chocolat
uhn pahn o shokolah
chocolate croissant

De la confiture
duh lah kohnfitewr
marmalade

du miel
dew myayl
honey

des œufs brouillés
dayzuh brooyay
scrambled eggs

un œuf à la coque
uhn nuhf ah lah kok
boiled egg

un œuf poché
uhn nuhf pohshay
poached egg

un yaourt aux fruits
uhn yaoort oh frwee
fruit yogurt

des fruits frais
day frwee fray
fresh fruit

FIRST COURSES

une soupe
ewn soop
soup

une soupe
de poisson
*ewn soop duh
pwassohn*
fish soup

un soufflé
uhn sooflay
soufflé

une piperade
ewn peepuhrad
piperade

du saumon fumé
*dew sohmohn
fewmay*
**smoked
salmon**

un consommé
uhn kohnsomay
broth/clear soup

une quiche
ewn keesh
savory tart

une omelette
ewn omlet
omelet

des œufs en
cocotte
*dayzuh ohn
kokot*
baked eggs

du jambon cru
*dew johnbohn
krew*
cured ham

des escargots
day zayskargo
snails

des rillettes
day reeyet
rillettes

des crevettes
grillées
*day kruhvet
greeyay*
grilled shrimp

des coquilles
Saint-Jacques
*day kokeey
sahn jak*
scallops

une assiette de
charcuterie
*ewn assyet duh
sharkewtree*
cold meats

des moules
au vin blanc
*day mool oh
vahn blohn*
**mussels
in white wine**

une tomate
farcie
*ewn tomat
farsee*
stuffed tomato

une salade au
chèvre chaud
*ewn salad
oh shayvr sho*
**goat's cheese
salad**

une salade
aux épinards
*ewn salad
ozaypeenar*
spinach salad

de l'aïoli
duh layolee
aioli

MAIN COURSES

I would like...	Je voudrais... *juh voodray*	...the turkey	...la dinde *lah dahnd*
...the lamb	...l'agneau *lanyo*	...the duck	...le canard *luh kanar*
...the pork	...le porc *luh por*	...the lobster	...le homard *luh ohmar*
...the beef	...le bœuf *luh buhf*	...the salmon	...le saumon *luh somohn*
...the steak	...le steak *luh stayk*	...the rabbit	...le lapin *luh lapahn*
...the ham	...le jambon *luh johnbohn*	roasted	rôti/rôtie *rohtee*
...the veal	...le veau *luh voh*	baked	au four *oh foor*
...the chicken	...le poulet *luh poolay*	broiled	grillé/grillée *greeyay*
...the pheasant	...le faisan *luh fuhzohn*	fried	frit/frite *free/freet*

YOU MAY SEE...

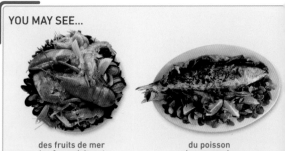

des fruits de mer
day frwee duh mair
seafood

du poisson
dew pwassohn
fish

YOU MAY HEAR...

Quelle cuisson, pour le steak?
kel kweesohn poor luh stayk
**How do you like
your steak?**

Saignant ou rosé?
saynyohn oo rohzay
Rare or medium rare?

Bien cuit?
byahn kwee
Well done?

steamed	à la vapeur *ah lah vapuhr*		**stewed**	en ragoût *ah laytewvay*
poached	poché/pochée *pohshay*		**stuffed**	farci/farcie *farsee*

de la volaille
duh lah volaeey
poultry

de la viande
duh lah vyohnd
meat

SALADS AND SIDE DISHES

une salade verte
ewn salad vairt
green salad

une salade mixte
ewn salad meext
mixed salad

de la purée de pommes de terre
duh lah pewray duh pom duh tair
mashed potato

des légumes à la vapeur
day laygewm ah lah vapuhr
steamed vegetables

des pâtes
day paht
pasta

du riz
dew ree
rice

des frites
day freet
French fries

du taboulé
dew taboolay
couscous

un tian provençal
uhn teeyohn prohvohnsal
Provençal vegetables

de la ratatouille
duh lah ratatoowee
ratatouille

DESERTS

un sorbet
uhn sorbay
sherbet

une glace
ewn glass
ice cream

un gâteau
uhn gato
cake

un baba au rhum
uhn baba oh rom
rum baba

une mousse
au chocolat
*ewn moos oh
shokolah*
**chocolate
mousse**

une crème
caramel
*ewn kraym
karamayl*
crème caramel

des crêpes
day krayp
crêpes

une crème brûlée
ewn kraym brewlay
crème brûlée

une tarte
aux fruits
*ewn tart oh
frwee*
fruit tart

une tarte
tatin
*ewn tart
tatahn*
**upside-down
apple tart**

PLACES TO STAY

France has a wide range of places to stay, depending on your personal preference and budget. These range from elegant *hôtels* and historic *châteaux* to smaller, family-run establishments and B & B-style *chambres d'hôtes*. If you want a self-catering option, you can rent a seaside villa, a *gîte* – a house in the country – or find a campsite to park your camper van or put up your tent.

MAKING A RESERVATION

I'd like...	Je voudrais... *juh voodray*
...to make a reservation	...réserver *rayzairvay*
...a double room	...une chambre pour deux personnes *ewn shohnbr poor duh pairson*
...a room with two twin beds	...une chambre à lits jumeaux *ewn shohnbr ah lee jewmoh*
...a single room	...une chambre individuelle *ewn shohnbr ahndeeveedewel*
...a family room	...une chambre familiale *ewn shohnbr fameelyal*
...a disabled person's room	...une chambre adaptée pour les handicapés *ewn shohnbr adaptay poor lay zohndeekapay*
...with a bathtub/shower	...avec baignoire/douche *avek baynwar/doosh*
...with a sea view	...avec vue sur la mer *avek vew sewr lah mair*
...for two nights	...pour deux nuits *poor duh nwee*
...for a week	...pour une semaine *poor ewn suhmen*
Is breakfast included?	Le petit-déjeuner est compris? *luh puhtee dayjuhnay ay kohnpree*
How much is it...	C'est combien... *say kombyahn*
...per night?	...par nuit? *par nwee*
...per week?	...par semaine? *par suhmen*

CHECKING IN

I have a reservation in the name of...	J'ai réservé au nom de... *jay rayzairvay oh nohn duh*
Do you have...	Vous avez... *voozavay*
I'd like...	Je voudrais... *juh voodray*
...the keys for room...	...les clés de la chambre... *lay klay duh la shohnbr*
...a wake-up call at...	...être réveillé à... *aytr rayvayay ah*
What time is...	À quelle heure est... *ah kel uhr ay*
...breakfast?	...le petit déjeuner? *luh puhtee dayjuhnay*
...dinner?	...le dîner? *luh deenay*

un bagagiste
uhn bagajist
porter

le minibar
luh meeneebar
mini bar

le service en chambre
luh sairvees ohn shohnbr
room service

les ascenseurs
lay zasohnsuhr
elevators

IN YOUR ROOM

Do you have...	Vous avez... *voo zavay*
another...	un/une autre... *uhn/ewn otruh*
some more...	d'autres... *dotruh*
I've lost my key	J'ai perdu ma clé *jay pairdew mah klay*

des couvertures
day koovairtewr
blankets

des oreillers
day zohrayay
pillows

un adaptateur
uhn ahdahptahtuhr
adapter

une ampoule
ewn ohnpool
light bulb

YOU MAY HEAR...

Votre chambre est le numéro...
votruh shohnbr ay luh newmairo
Your room number is...

Voici votre clé
vwasee votruh klay
Here is your key

IN THE HOTEL

The room is...	La chambre est... *lah shohnbr ay*
...too hot	...trop chaude *tro shohd*
...too cold	...trop froide *tro frwad*
The TV doesn't work	La télé ne marche pas *lah taylay nuh marshuh pa*
The window won't open	La fenêtre n'ouvre pas *lah fuhnaytr noovruh pa*
What is the code for the wifi?	Quel est le code pour le wifi? *kel ay luh kod poor luh weefee*

la bouilloire
lah booywar
kettle

le radiateur
luh rahdeeyatuhr
radiator

le thermostat
luh tairmosta
thermostat

la chambre
individuelle
*lah shohnbr
ahndeeveedewel*
single room

la chambre
double
*lah shohnbr
doobluh*
double room

le numéro
de chambre
*luh newmayro
duh shohnbr*
room number

le téléviseur
luh taylayveezuhr
television

la télécommande
lah taylaykomohnd
remote control

le cintre
luh sahntr
coat hanger

le store
luh stohr
Venetian blind

CHECKING OUT

When do I have to vacate the room?	À quelle heure faut-il quitter la chambre? *ah kel uhr foteel keetay lah shohnbr*
Is there a porter to carry my bags?	Y a-t-il un bagagiste pour mes sacs? *eeyateel uhn bagajist poor may sak*
May I have the bill please?	Je peux avoir la note, s'il vous plaît? *juh puh avwar lah noht seel voo play*
Can I pay...	Je peux payer... *juh puh payay*
...by credit card?	...par carte de crédit? *par kart duh kraydee*
...cash?	...en liquide? *ohn leekeed*
I'd like a receipt	Je voudrais un reçu *juh voodray uhn ruhsew*

IN THE BATHROOM

les serviettes
lay sairvyet
towels

le peignoir
luh paynwar
bathrobe

le savon
luh savohn
soap

le déodorant
luh dayodorohn
deodorant

le dentifrice
luh dohnteefrees
toothpaste

le bain moussant
luh bahn moosohn
bubblebath

le bidet
luh beeday
bidet

le gel douche
luh jel doosh
shower gel

la baignoire
lah baynwar
bathtub

le lait corps
luh lay kohr
body lotion

la brosse à dents
lah bros ah dohn
toothbrush

le sèche-cheveux
luh saysh shuhvuh
blow-dryer

le rasoir électrique
luh razwar aylayktreek
electric razor

la mousse à raser
lah moos ah razay
shaving foam

le rasoir
luh razwar
razor

le bain de bouche
luh bahn duh boosh
mouthwash

le shampooing
luh shohnpooahn
shampoo

l'après-shampooing
lapray shohnpooahn
conditioner

le coupe-ongles
luh koopohngluh
nail clippers

les ciseaux à ongles
lay seezo ah ohngluh
nail scissors

SELF-CATERING

May we have...	On peut avoir... *ohn puh avwar*
...the key, please?	...la clé, s'il vous plaît? *lah klay seel voo play*
...an extra bed?	...un lit supplémentaire? *uhn lee sewplaymohntair*
...a child's bed?	...un lit d'enfant? *uhn lee dohnfohn*
...more cutlery?	...d'autres couverts? *dotruh koovair*
...more dishes?	...plus de vaisselle? *plew duh vaysel*
Where is...	Où se trouve... *oo suh troov*
...the fusebox?	...la boîte à fusibles? *lah bwat ah fewzeebl*

le convecteur
luh kohnvektuhr
space heater

le ventilateur
luh vohnteelatuhr
fan

le lit bébé
uh lee baybay
crib

la chaise haute
lah shayz oht
high chair

...the water valve? — ...l'arrivée d'eau?
lareevay do

...the supermarket? — ...le supermarché?
luh sewpairmarshay

...the nearest store? — ...le magasin le plus proche?
luh magahzahn luh plew prosh

Do you do babysitting? — Vous gardez les enfants?
voo gahrday lay zohnfohn

How does the heating work? — Comment marche le chauffage?
kohmohn marsh luh shofaj

Is there... — Y a-t-il...
eeyateel

...air-conditioning? — ...la climatisation?
lah klimateezasyohn

...central heating? — ...le chauffage central?
luh shofaj sohntral

When does the cleaner come? — À quelle heure vient la femme de ménage?
ah kel uhr vyahn lah fahm duh maynaj

Where do I put the garbage? — Où faut-il mettre les déchets?
oo foteel maytruh lay dayshay

Do you allow pets? — Vous acceptez les animaux?
voo zaksayptay lay zaneemo

le chien
luh shyahn
dog

IN THE VILLA OR GÎTE

Is there an inventory?	Il y a un inventaire? *eeleeya uhn ahnvohntair*
Where is this item?	Où se trouve cet objet? *oo suh troov set objay*
I need...	Il me faut... *eel muh fo*
...an adapter	...un adaptateur *uhn ahdahptahtuhr*
...an extension cord	...une rallonge *ewn ralohnj*
...a flashlight	...une lampe torche *ewn lohnp torsh*
...matches	...des allumettes *day zalewmet*

le micro-ondes
luh meekro-ohnd
microwave

le fer à repasser
luh fair ah ruhpassay
iron

la planche à repasser
*lah plohnsh
ah ruhpassay*
ironing board

la serpillère et le seau
lah sairpeeyair ay luh so
mop and bucket

la pelle et le balai
lah pel ay luh balay
dustpan and brush

le produit de nettoyage
*luh prodwee
duh netwayaj*
detergent

The shower doesn't work

La douche ne marche pas
lah doosh nuh marshuh pa

The toilet is leaking

Les toilettes fuient
lay twalet fwee

Can you fix it today?

Vous pouvez faire les réparations
aujourd'hui?
*voo poovay fair lay rayparasyohn
ojoordwee*

There's no...

Il n'y a pas...
eel neeya pa

...electricity

...d'électricité
daylektreeseetay

...water

...d'eau
doh

la machine à laver
lah masheen ah lahvay
washing machine

le réfrigérateur
luh rayfreejayratuhr
refrigerator

l'extincteur
lextahnktuhr
fire extinguisher

la serrure et les clés
lah sairewr ay lay klay
lock and keys

le détecteur de fumée
luh daytayktuhr duh fewmay
smoke alarm

la poubelle
lah poobel
trash can

KITCHEN EQUIPMENT

la planche à découper
lah plohnsh ah daykoopay
cutting board

la plaque à four
lah plak a foor
cookie sheet

le fouet
luh fooeh
whisk

le couteau de cuisine
luh kooto duh kweezeen
kitchen knife

l'économiseur
laykonomeezuhr
peeler

l'ouvre-boîte
loovruh bwat
can opener

le décapsuleur
luh daykapsewluhr
bottle opener

le tire-bouchon
luh teer booshohn
corkscrew

la râpe
lah rap
grater

la cuiller en bois
lah kweeyair ohn bwa
wooden spoon

la poêle
lah pwal
frying pan

la passoire
lah paswar
colander

la spatule
lah spatewl
spatula

la casserole
lah kasrohl
saucepan

le gril
luh greel
griddle pan

la marmite
lah marmeet
casserole dish

le bol mélangeur
luh bohl maylohnjuhr
mixing bowl

le tablier
luh tableeyay
apron

le gant de cuisine
luh gohn duh kweezeen
oven mitts

le mixeur
luh meexuhr
blender

CAMPING

Where is the nearest...	Où se trouve le...le plus proche... *oo suh troov luh plew prosh*
...campsite?	...terrain de camping? *tairahn duh kohnpeeng*
...camper van site?	...camping pour caravanes? *kohping poor kahrahvan*
Can we camp here?	On peut camper ici? *ohn puh kohnpay eesee*
Do you have any vacancies?	Il y a de la place? *eeleeya duh lah plass*
What is the charge...	C'est combien... *say kombyahn*
...per night?	...par nuit? *par nwee*
...per week?	...par semaine? *par suhmen*
Does the price include...	Le prix inclut... *luh pree ahnklew*
...electricity?	...l'électricité? *laylektreeseetay*
...hot water?	...l'eau chaude? *lo shohd*
Are showers extra?	Les douches sont en plus? *lay doosh sohn tohn plews*
We want to stay for...	Nous voulons rester... *noo voolohn restay*

la tente
lah tohnt
tent

le tendeur
luh tohnduhr
guy rope

Can I rent...	On peut louer... *ohn puh looay*
...a tent?	...une tente? *ewn tohnt*
...a bicycle?	...des vélos? *day vaylo*
...a barbecue?	...un barbecue? *uhn barbuhkyoo*
Where are...	Où sont... *oo sohn*
...the restrooms?	...les toilettes? *lay twalet*
...the garbage cans?	...les poubelles? *lay poobel*
Are there...	Il y a... *eeleeya*
...showers?	...des douches? *day doosh*
...laundry facilities?	...une laverie? *ewn lahvree*
Is there...	Il y a... *eeleeya*
...a swimming pool?	...une piscine? *ewn peeseen*
...a store?	...un magasin? *uhn magazahn*

YOU MAY HEAR...

Ne faites pas de feu
nuh fet pah duh fuh
Don't light a fire

Ne buvez pas l'eau
nuh bewvay pah lo
Don't drink the water

AT THE CAMPSITE

le panier à
pique-nique
*uh panyay
ah peek neek*
picnic basket

la bouteille
thermos
*lah bootayeey
tairmos*
vacuum flask

a bouilloire
de camping
*lah booywar
duh kohnpeeng*
camping kettle

les imperméables
lay zahnpairmayably
slickers

l'eau en bouteilles
lo ohn bootayeey
bottled water

le réchaud
luh raysho
camping stove

la glacière
lah glasyair
cooler

le barbecue
luh barbuhkyoo
barbecue

le matelas gonflable
luh matla gohnflabl
air mattress

le sac de
couchage
*luh sak duh
kooshaj*
sleeping bag

la lampe torche
lah lohnp torsh
flashlight

le sac à dos
luh sakado
backpack

le seau
luh so
bucket

le maillet
luh mayay
mallet

le produit contre
les insectes
*luh prodwee kohntr
layzahnsekt*
insect repellent

la crème solaire
lah kraym solair
sunscreen

le pansement
luh pohnsmohn
**adhesive
bandage**

la pelote
de ficelle
*lah puhlot
duh feesell*
ball of string

les chaussures
de marche
*lay shosewr
duh marsh*
hiking boots

la boussole
lah boosol
compass

SHOPPING

As well as department stores, hypermarkets and specialist shops, France has many picturesque open-air markets in town squares and high streets where you can buy food, clothes and even antiques relatively cheaply. Most shops are open between 9.00am and 6.30pm from Monday to Saturday, but some stores and food shops close on Mondays, and in small towns and villages they often close for two hours for lunch.

IN THE STORE

I'm looking for...	Je cherche... *juh shairsh*
Do you have...?	Vous avez...? *voo zavay*
I'm just looking	Je regarde *juh ruhgard*
I'm being served	On s'occupe de moi *ohn sokewp duh mwa*
Do you have any more of these?	Vous en avez d'autres? *voo zohn navay dohtr*
How much is this?	C'est combien? *say kombyahn*
Have you anything cheaper?	Vous avez des articles moins chers? *voo zavay day zarteekl mwahn shair*
I'll take this one	Je prends ça *juh prohn sah*
Where can I pay?	Où sont les caisses? *oo sohn lay kess*
I'll pay...	Je paye... *juh payuh*
...in cash	...en liquide *ohn leekeed*
...by credit card	...par carte de crédit *par kart duh kraydee*
May I have a receipt?	Je peux avoir un reçu? *juh puh avwar uhn ruhsew*
I'd like to exchange this	Je voudrais échanger cet article *juh voodray ayshohnjay set arteekl*

IN THE BANK

I'd like...	Je voudrais... *juh voodray*
...to make a withdrawal	...retirer de l'argent *ruhteeray duh larjohn*
...to deposit some money	...déposer de l'argent *dayposay duh larjohn*
...to change some money	...faire du change *fair dew shohnj*
...into euros	...en euros *ohn nuhro*
...into dollars/sterling	...en dollars/livres sterling *ohn dohllars/leevruh stairling*
Here is my passport	Voici mon passeport *vwasee mohn passpor*
My name is...	Je m'appelle... *juh mahpel*
My account number is...	Mon numéro de compte est le... *mohn newmairo duh kohnt ay luh*
My bank details are...	Voici mes coordonnées bancaires... *vwasee may ko-ordonay bohnkair*

le passeport
luh passpor
passport

l'argent
larjohn
money

le taux de change
luh toh duh shohnj
exchange rate

Do I have...	Il faut... *eel fo*
...to key in my PIN?	...entrer son code secret? *ohntray sohn kohd suhkray*
...to sign here?	...signer ici? *seenyay eesee*
Is there a cash machine?	Il y a un distributeur? *eeleeya uhn deestreebewtuhr*
The cash machine has swallowed my card	Le distributeur a avalé ma carte *luh deestreebewtuhr a ahvahlay mah kart*
Can I cash a check?	Je peux encaisser un chèque? *juh puh ohnkessay uhn shek*
Has my money arrived yet?	Mon argent est arrivé? *mohn narjohn ayt ahreevay*
When does the bank open/close?	À quelle heure ouvre/ferme la banque? *ah kel uhr oovr/fairm lah bohnk*

le distributeur
luh deestreebewtuhr
cash machine

la carte de crédit
lah kart duh kraydee
credit card

le carnet de chèques
luh karnay duh shek
checkbook

STORES

le marchand de légumes
luh marshohn duh laygewm
produce stand

la poissonnerie
lah pwassonree
fish seller

l'épicerie
laypeesree
grocery

la charcuterie
lah sharkewtree
delicatessen

la boulangerie
lah boolohnjree
bakery

la librairie
lah leebrairee
bookstore

le supermarché
luh sewpairmarshay
supermarket

la boucherie
lah booshree
butcher

le bureau de tabac
luh bewro duh taba
tobacconist

le magasin de
meubles
*luh magahzahn
duh muhbl*
furniture store

le magasin de chaussures
luh magahzahn duh shohsewr
shoe store

la boutique
lah booteek
boutique

la bijouterie
lah beejootree
jewelry store

la quincaillerie
lah kahnkahyuhree
hardware store

le tailleur
luh tayuhr
tailor

AT THE MARKET

I would like...	Je voudrais... *juh voodray*
How much is this?	C'est combien? *say kombyahn*
What's the price per kilo?	C'est combien au kilo? *say kombyahn oh keelo*
It's too expensive	C'est trop cher *say tro shair*
That's fine, I'll take it	C'est bon, je le prends *say bohn juh luh prohn*
I'll take two kilos	Deux kilos, s'il vous plaît *duh keelo seel voo play*
A kilo of...	Un kilo de... *uhn keelo duh*
Half a kilo of...	Une livre de... *ewn leevr duh*
A little more, please	Un peu plus, s'il vous plaît *uhn puh plews seel voo play*
May I taste it?	Je peux goûter? *juh puh gootay*
That's very good. I'll take some	C'est très bon. J'en prends *say tray bohn john prohn*
That will be all, thank you	C'est tout, merci *say too mairsee*

YOU MAY HEAR...

Vous désirez? *voo dayzeeray* May I help you?	Vous en voulez combien? *voo zohn voolay kombyahn* How much would you like?

IN THE SUPERMARKET

Where is/are...	Où se trouve/trouvent...
	oo suh troov/troov
...the frozen foods	...les surgelés?
	leh sewrjuhlay
...the beverage aisle?	...le rayon des boissons?
	luh rayohn day bwasohn
...the checkout?	...les caisses?
	lay kess
I'm looking for...	Je cherche...
	juh shairsh

le chariot
luh shahreeyo
grocery cart

le panier
luh panyay
basket

Do you have any more?	Il vous en reste?
	eel voo zohn rest
Is this reduced?	C'est en promotion?
	say tohn promosyohn
Can you help me pack	Vous pouvez m'aider à mettre les articles dans les sacs?
	voo poovay mayday ah maytruh layzarteekl dohn lay sak
Where do I pay?	Je paye où?
	juh pay oo
Shall I key in my PIN?	J'entre mon code secret?
	johntruh mohn kod suhkray
May I have a bag?	Je peux avoir un sac?
	juh puh avwar uhn sak

FRUIT

une orange
ewn orohnj
orange

un citron
uhn seetrohn
lemon

une pêche
ewn paysh
peach

une nectarine
ewn nayktareen
nectarine

un citron vert
uhn seetrohn vair
lime

des cerises
day suhreez
cherries

un abricot
uhn nabreeko
apricot

une prune
ewn prewn
plum

un pamplemousse
uhn pohnpluhmooss
grapefruit

des myrtilles
day meerteeyuh
blueberries

une fraise
ewn frayz
strawberry

une framboise
ewn frohnbwaz
raspberry

un melon
uhn muhlohn
melon

du raisin
dew rayzahn
grapes

une banane
ewn banan
banana

une grenade
ewn gruhnad
pomegranate

une pomme
ewn pom
apple

une poire
ewn pwar
pear

un ananas
uhn nananas
pineapple

une mangue
ewn mohng
mango

VEGETABLES

une pomme
de terre
ewn pom duh tair
potato

des carottes
day karots
carrots

un poivron
uhn pwavrohn
pepper

des piments
day peemohn
chili peppers

une aubergine
ewn obairjeen
egg plant

une tomate
ewn tomat
tomato

un oignon
uhn onyohn
onion

de l'ail
duh laeey
garlic

un oignon vert
uhn onyohn vair
scallion

un poireau
uhn pwaro
leek

des champignons
day shohnpeenyohn
mushrooms

une courgette
ewn koorjet
zucchini

des petits pois
day puhtee pwa
garden peas

des haricots verts
day areeko vair
green beans

un concombre
uhn kohnkohnbr
cucumber

du céleri
dew saylayree
celery

des épinards
dayzaypeenar
spinach

du brocoli
dew brokolee
broccoli

une laitue
ewn laytew
lettuce

un chou
uhn shoo
cabbage

MEAT AND POULTRY

May I have...	Je peux avoir... *juh puh avwar*
...a slice of...?	...une tranche de...? *ewn trohnsh duh*
...a piece of...?	...un morceau de...? *uhn morso duh*

du jambon
dew johnbohn
ham

de la viande
hachée
*duh lah
vyohnd ashay*
ground beef

un steak
uhn stayk
steak

un filet
uhn feelay
fillet

une côte
ewn kot
chop

un gigot
d'agneau
*uhn jeego
danyo*
leg of lamb

du poulet
dew poolay
chicken

du canard
dew kanar
duck

FISH AND SHELLFISH

de la dorade
duh lah dorad
sea bream

du saumon
dew somohn
salmon

de la truite
duh lah trweet
trout

du bar
dew bar
sea bass

du cabillaud
dew kabeeyo
cod

des sardines
day sardeen
sardines

du crabe
dew krab
crab

un homard
uhn omar
lobster

des coquilles
Saint-Jacques
*day kokeey
sahn jak*
scallops

des crevettes
day kruhvet
shrimp

BREAD AND CAKES

un petit pain
*uhn puhtee
pahn*
roll

une baguette
ewn baget
French stick

du pain
au levain
*dew pahn
oh luhvahn*
sourdough bread

de la brioche
duh lah breeosh
brioche

un croissant
uhn krwassohn
croissant

un pain au
chocolat
*uhn pahn
oh shokolah*
**chocolate
croissant**

une tarte au citron
ewn tart oh seetrohn
lemon tart

un éclair au chocolat
uhn ayclair oh shokolah
chocolate éclair

une tarte
aux fruits
*ewn tart
oh frwee*
fruit tart

des madeleines
day madlayn
sponge cakes

DAIRY PRODUCE

du lait entier
dew lay ohntyay
whole milk

du lait
demi-écrémé
*dew lay duhmee
aykraymay*
reduced-fat milk

du camembert
dew kamohnbair
camembert

du fromage râpé
dew fromaj rapay
grated cheese

du yaourt
dew yaoort
yogurt

du beurre
dew buhr
butter

de la crème
fraîche
*duh lah
kraym fraysh*
crème fraîche

de la crème
liquide
*duh lah
kraym leekeed*
half-and-half

du lait de chèvre
dew lay duh shayvr
goat's milk

du fromage
de chèvre
*dew fromaj
duh shayvr*
goat's cheese

NEWSPAPERS AND MAGAZINES

Do you have...	Vous avez... *voo zavay*
...any more postcards?	...d'autres cartes postales? *dohtr kart postal*
...a book of stamps?	...des timbres? *day tahnbr*
...airmail stamps?	...des timbres par avion? *day tahnbr par avyohn*
...a pack of envelopes?	...un paquet d'enveloppes? *uhn pakay dohnvlop*
...some adhesive tape?	...du scotch? *dew scotch*

une carte postale
ewn kart postal
postcard

un crayon
uhn krayohn
pencil

des timbres
day tahnbr
stamps

un stylo
uhn steelo
pen

YOU MAY HEAR...

Vous avez quel âge?
voo zavay kel aj
How old are you?

Vous avez une carte d'identité?
voo zavay ewn kart deedohnteetay
Do you have ID?

I'd like...

Je voudrais...
juh voodray

...a pack of cigarettes

...un paquet de cigarettes
uhn pakay duh seegaret

...a box of matches

...des allumettes
deh zalewmet

une BD
ewn bayday
comic book

un briquet
uhn breekay
lighter

des crayons de couleur
day krayohn duh kooluhr
colored pencils

des chewing-gums
day shuhweengom
chewing gum

des bonbons
day bohnbohn
candy

du tabac
dew taba
tobacco

un magazine
uhn magazeen
magazine

un journal
uhn joornal
newspaper

BUYING CLOTHES AND SHOES

I am looking for...	Je cherche... *juh shairsh*
I am size...	Je fais du *juh fay dew*
Do you have this...	Vous avez celui-là... *voo zavay suhlwee lah*
...in my size?	...dans ma taille? *dohn ma taeey*
...in small?	...en S? *luh mem ohn es*
...in medium?	...en M? *luh mem ohn em*
...in large?	...en L? *luh mem ohn el*
...in other colors?	...dans d'autres couleurs? *dohn dohtr kooluhr*
May I try this on?	Je peux essayer? *juh puh aysayay*
I'll take this one	Je prends celui-là *juh prohn suhlwee lah*
It's...	C'est... *say*
...too big	...trop grand *troh grohn*
...too small	...trop petit *troh puhtee*
I need...	Il me faut... *eel muh fo*
...a larger size	...la taille au-dessus *lah taeey oh duhsew*
...a smaller size	...la taille en dessous *lah taeey ohn duhsoo*

| I take shoe size... | Je fais du... |
| | *juh fay dew* |

| May I try... | Je peux essayer... |
| | *juh puh aysayay* |

| ...this pair? | ...cette paire? |
| | *set pair* |

| ...those in the window? | ...celles de la vitrine? |
| | *sel duh lah veetreen* |

| These are... | Elles sont... |
| | *el sohn* |

| ...too tight | ...trop serrées |
| | *troh sairay* |

| ...too big | ...trop grandes |
| | *troh grohnd* |

| ...too small | ...trop petites |
| | *troh puhteet* |

| ...uncomfortable | ...inconfortables |
| | *ahnkohnfortabl* |

| Is there a bigger size? | Vous avez la pointure au-dessus? |
| | *voo zavay lah pwahntewr o duhsew* |

| ...a smaller size? | ...la pointure en dessous? |
| | *lah pwahntewr ohn duhsoo* |

CLOTHES AND SHOE SIZES GUIDE

Women's clothes sizes	US	4	6	8	10	12	14	16	18	
	Europe	34	36	38	40	42	44	46	48	
Men's clothes sizes	US	36	38	40	42	44	46	48	50	
	Europe	46	48	50	52	54	56	58	60	
Shoe sizes	US	5	6	7	8	9	10	11	12	13
	Europe	36	37	38	39	40	42	43	45	46

CLOTHES AND SHOES

une robe
ewn rob
dress

une robe de soirée
ewn rob duh swaray
evening dress

une veste
ewn vest
jacket

un pull
uhn pewl
sweater

un jean
uhn djeen
jeans

une jupe
ewn jewp
skirt

des tennis
day taynis
sneakers

des bottes
day bot
boots

un sac à main
uhn sak a mahn
handbag

une ceinture
ewn sahntewr
belt

le costume
luh kostewm
suit

l'imperméable
lahnpairmayabl
coat

une chemise
ewn shuhmeez
shirt

un t-shirt
uhn teeshuhrt
T-shirt

un short
uhn short
shorts

des sandales à
talons
*day sohndal ah
talohn*
sandals

des chaussures
de ville
*day shosewr
duh veel*
tie shoes

des chaussures
à talons
*day shosewr ah
talohn*
**high-heeled
shoes**

des tongs
day tohng
flip-flops

des chaussettes
day shoset
socks

AT THE GIFT SHOP

I'd like to buy a gift for...	Je cherche un cadeau pour... *juh shairsh uhn kado poor*
...my mother/father	...ma mère/mon père *ma mair/mohn pair*
...my daughter/son	...ma fille/mon fils *ma feeyuh/mohn fees*
...a child	...un enfant *uhn nohnfohn*
...a friend	...un ami/une amie *uhn namee/ewn amee*
Can you recommend something?	Vous pouvez me conseiller quelque chose? *voo poovay muh kohnsayay kelkuh shoz*
Do you have a box for it?	Vous avez une boîte? *voo zavay ewn bwat*
Can you gift-wrap it?	Vous pouvez me faire un paquet-cadeau? *voo poovay muh fair uhn pakay kado*

un bracelet
uhn brasslay
bracelet

des boutons de manchette
day bootohn duh mohnshet
cufflinks

un collier
uhn kolyay
necklace

une montre
ewn mohntr
watch

un portefeuille
uhn portuhfuhy
wallet

une poupée
ewn poopay
doll

une peluche
ewn puhlewsh
stuffed animal

des chocolats
day shokolah
chocolates

I want a souvenir of...	Je cherche un souvenir de... *juh shairsh uhn soovuhneer duh*
Is there a guarantee?	Il y a une garantie? *eeleeya ewn garohntee*
May I exchange this?	C'est échangeable en cas de problème? *set ayshohnjabl ohn ka duh problaym*

YOU MAY HEAR...

C'est pour offrir?
say poor ofreer
Is it for a present?

Vous voulez un paquet-cadeau?
voo voolay uhn pakay kado
Shall I gift-wrap it?

PHOTOGRAPHY

I'd like this film developed	Je voudrais faire développer cette pellicule *juh voodray fair dayvlohpay sayt payleekewl*
When will it be ready?	Ça sera prêt quand? *sah suhra pray kohn*
Do you have an express service?	Vous avez un service rapide? *voo zavay uhn sairvees rapeed*
I'd like...	Je voudrais... *juh voodray*

un appareil photo numérique
uhn naparayeey foto newmaireek
digital camera

une carte mémoire
ewn kart maymwar
memory card

un cadre
uhn kadr
photo frame

un album photo
uhn nalbuhm foto
photo album

...the one-hour service

...le service de développement
en une heure
*luh servees duh dayvlopmohn
ohn ewn uhr*

**Can you print from this
memory stick?**

Vous pouvez imprimer à partir
de cette clé USB?
*voo poovay ahnpreemay ah parteer
duh sayt kart*

un objectif
uhn nobjaykteef
lens

un appareil photo
uhn naparayeey foto
camera

un étui
uhn naytwee
camera bag

un flash
uhn flash
flash gun

YOU MAY HEAR...

Quelle taille préférez-vous?
kel taeey prayfairay voo
What size prints do you want?

Mat ou brillant?
mat oo breeyohn
Matte or gloss?

Vous les voulez quand?
voo lay voolay kohn
When do you want them?

AT THE POST OFFICE

I'd like...	Je voudrais... *juh voodray*
...three stamps, please	...trois timbres, s'il vous plaît *trwa tahnbr seel voo play*
...to register this letter	...envoyer cette lettre en recommandé *ohnvwayay set laytr ohn ruhkomohnday*
...to send this airmail	...envoyer ça par avion *ohnvwayay sah par avyohn*

des timbres
day tahnbr
stamps

une enveloppe
ewn ohnvlop
envelope

par avion
par avyohn
airmail

une carte postale
ewn kart postahl
postcard

YOU MAY HEAR...

Quel est le contenu ?
kel ay luh kohntuhnew
What are the contents?

Quelle est sa valeur ?
kel ay sah valuhr
What is their value?

| How much is...? | Combien ça coûte pour...? |
| | *kombyahn sah koot poor* |

| ...a letter to... | ...une lettre pour... |
| | *ewn laytr poor* |

| ...a postcard to... | ...une carte postale pour... |
| | *ewn kart postal poor* |

| ...the United States | ...les États-Unis |
| | *lay zayta zewnee* |

| ...Great Britain | la Grande-Bretagne |
| | *la grohnd bruhtanyuh* |

| ...Canada | ...le Canada |
| | *luh kanada* |

| ...Australia | ...l'Australie |
| | *lohstrahlee* |

| May I have a receipt? | Je peux avoir un reçu? |
| | *juh puh avwar uhn ruhsew* |

| Where can I mail this? | Je poste ça où? |
| | *juh post sah oo* |

un paquet
uhn pakay
package

le coursier
luh koorsyay
courier

la boîte aux lettres
la bwat oh laytr
mailbox

le facteur
luh faktuhr
letter carrier

TELEPHONES

Who's speaking?	Qui est à l'appareil? *kee aytah laparayeey*
Hello, this is...	Allô, c'est... *alo, say*
I'd like to speak to...	Je voudrais parler à... *juh voodray parlay ah*
May I leave a message?	Je peux laisser un message? *juh puh laysay uhn messaj*
Where is the nearest phone shop?	Où se trouve la boutique de téléphones portables la plus proche? *oo suh troov lah booteek duh taylayfon portabl lah plew prosh*

le téléphone sans fil
luh taylayfon sohn feel
cordless phone

le smartphone
luh smartfon
smartphone

le téléphone portable
luh taylayfon portabl
cell phone

le répondeur
luh raypohnduhr
answering machine

la cabine à pièces
lah kabeen ah pyayss
coin-operated phone

INTERNET

Is there an internet café near here?
Il y a un cybercafé près d'ici?
eeleeya uhn seebairkafay pray deesee

How much do you charge?
C'est combien?
say kombyahn

Do you have wireless internet?
Vous avez une connexion wifi?
voo zavay ewn koneksyohn weefee

Can I check my emails?
Je peux regarder mes e-mails?
juh puh ruhgarday may zeemail

I need to send an email
Je dois envoyer un e-mail
juh dwa ohnvwayay uhn email

What's your email address?
Quelle est ton adresse e-mail?
kel ay tohn nadrays email

My email address is...
Mon adresse e-mail est...
mohn nadrays email ay

Can I send an email from here?
On peut envoyer des e-mails d'ici?
ohn puh ohnvwayay day zeemail deesee

l'ordinateur portable
lordeenatuhr portabl
laptop

le clavier
luh klavyay
keyboard

le site web
luh seet web
website

l'e-mail
leemail
email

SIGHTSEEING

In most towns, the tourist information office is
near the train station or town hall and the staff will
advise you on interesting local places to visit and
cultural events. Most of the national museums in
France close on Tuesdays as well as on public
holidays, so it is best to check the opening times
before visiting.

AT THE TOURIST OFFICE

Where is the tourist information office?
Où se trouve l'office du tourisme?
oo suh troov lofees dew tooreesm

Can you recommend...
Vous pouvez nous indiquer...
voo poovay noo zahndeekay

...a guided tour?
...une visite guidée?
ewn veezeet geeday

...an excursion?
...une excursion?
ewn exkewrsyohn

Is there a museum?
Il y a un musée?
eeleeya uhn mewzay

Is it open to the public?
C'est ouvert au public?
say toovair oh pewbleek

Is there wheelchair access?
Il y a un accès handicapés?
eeleeya uhn aksay ohndeekapay

Does it close...
Ça ferme...
sah fairm

...on Sundays?
...le dimanche?
luh deemohnsh

...on public holidays?
...les jours fériés?
lay joor fairyay

Do you have...
Vous avez...
voo zavay

...a street map?
...un plan de la ville?
uhn plohn duh lah veel

...a guide?
...un guide?
uhn geed

...any leaflets?
...des prospectus?
day prospektews

Can you show me on the map?
Vous pouvez me montrer sur le plan?
voo poovay muh mohntray sewr luh plohn

VISITING PLACES

What time...	À quelle heure... *ah kel uhr*
...do you open?	...ouvrez-vous? *oovray voo*
...do you close?	...fermez-vous? *fairmay voo*
I'd like two entrance tickets	Je voudrais deux entrées *juh voodray duh zohntray*
Two adults, please	Deux adultes, s'il vous plaît *duh zadewlt seel voo play*
A family ticket	Un billet famille *uhn beeyay fameel*
How much does it cost?	C'est combien? *say kombyahn*
Are there reductions...	Il y a une réduction... *eeleeya ewn raydewksyohn*
...for children?	...pour les enfants? *poor lay zohnfohn*
...for students?	...pour les étudiants? *poor lay zaytewdyohn*

le plan
luh plohn
street map

l'office du tourisme
lofees dew tooreesm
tourist office

le billet d'entrée
luh beeyay dohntray
entrance ticket

l'accès handicapés
laksay ohndeekapay
wheelchair access

Can I buy a guidebook?	Je peux acheter un guide? *juh puh ashuhtay uhn geed*
Is there...	Il y a... *eeleeya*
...an audio guide?	...un guide audio? *uhn geed audio*
...a guided tour?	...une visite guidée? *ewn veezeet geeday*
...an elevator?	...un ascenseur? *uhn asohnsuhr*
...a café?	...un café? *uhn kafay*
...a bus tour?	...une visite en bus? *ewn veezeet ohn bews*
When is the next tour?	À quelle heure est la prochaine visite? *ah kel uhr ay lah proshayn veezeet*

le bus touristique
luh bews tooreesteek
tour bus

YOU MAY HEAR...

Vous avez quel âge?
voo zavay kel aj
How old are you?

Vous avez une carte d'étudiant?
voo zavay ewn kart daytewdyohn
Do you have a student ID?

FINDING YOUR WAY

Excuse me	Excusez-moi *exkewzay mwa*
Can you help me?	Vous pouvez m'aider? *voo poovay mayday*
Is this the way to...?	C'est par là...? *say par lah*
How do I get to...	Pour aller... *poor allay*
...the town center?	...au centre-ville? *oh sohntruh veel*
...the station?	...à la gare? *ah lah gar*
...the museum?	...au musée? *oh mewzay*
Is it far?	C'est loin? *say lwahn*
Is it within walking distance?	On peut y aller à pied? *ohn puh ee allay ah peeyay*
Can you show me on the map?	Vous pouvez me montrer sur le plan? *voo poovay muh mohntray sewr luh plohn*

YOU MAY HEAR...

Ce n'est pas loin
suh nay pah lwahn
It's not far away

C'est à dix minutes
say tah dee meenewt
It takes ten minutes

Il faut prendre un bus
eel foh prohndr uhn bews
You need to take a bus

YOU MAY HEAR...

Nous sommes là
noo som lah
We are here

Prenez la première...
pruhney lah pruhmyair
Take the first...

Continuez tout droit...
kohnteeneway too drwa
Keep going straight...

...à gauche/à droite
ah gohsh/ah drwat
...on the left/right

...jusqu'au bout de la rue
jewsko boo duh lah rew
...to the end of the street

C'est devant
say duhvohn
It's in front of you

...jusqu'aux feux
jewsko fuh
...to the traffic lights

C'est derrière
say dairyair
It's behind you

...jusqu'à la grande place
jewska lah grohnd plas
...to the main square

C'est en face
say tohn fass
It's opposite you

Par ici
par eesee
This way

C'est à côté de...
say tah kotay duh
It's next to...

Par là
par lah
That way

C'est indiqué
say tahndeekay
It's signed

Tournez à droite à...
toornay ah drwat ah
Turn right at...

C'est par là
say par lah
It's over there

Tournez à gauche à...
oornay ah gohsh ah
Turn left at...

PLACES TO VISIT

la mairie
lah mairee
town hall

le pont
luh pohn
bridge

le musée
luh mewzay
museum

la galerie d'art
lah galree dar
art gallery

le monument
luh monewmohn
monument

l'église
laygleez
church

le village
luh veelaj
village

la cathédrale
lah kataydral
cathedral

le château
luh shato
castle

le phare
luh far
lighthouse

le port
luh por
harbor

le vignoble
luh veenyobl
vineyard

le parc
luh park
park

la côte
lah koht
coast

la cascade
lah kaskad
waterfall

les montagnes
lay mohntanyuh
mountains

OUTDOOR ACTIVITIES

Where can we go...	Où peut-on aller... *oo puh tonh allay*
...horseback riding?	...faire de l'équitation? *fair duh laykeetasyohn*
...fishing?	...pêcher? *payshay*
...swimming?	...nager? *najay*
...walking?	...faire de la randonnée? *fair duh lah rohndonay*
Can we...	On peut... *ohn puh*
...rent equipment?	...louer le matériel? *looay luh matairyayl*
...take lessons?	...prendre des cours? *prohndr day koor*
How much per hour?	C'est combien par heure? *say kombyahn par uhr*
I'm a beginner	Je suis débutant *juh swee daybewtohn*
I'm very experienced	J'ai pas mal d'expérience *jay pah mal dekspairyohns*
Where's the amusement park?	Où se trouve le parc d'attraction? *oo suh troov luh park datraksyohn*
Can the children go on all the rides?	Les enfants sont autorisés sur tous les manèges? *lay zohnfohn sohn totoreezay sewr too lay manayj*
Is there a playground?	Il y a une aire de jeux? *eeleeya ewn air duh juh*
Is it safe for children?	La sécurité est assurée pour les enfants? *lah saykewreetay etasewray poor lay zohnfohn*

le zoo
luh zoh
zoo

l'aire de jeux
lair duh juh
playground

le pique-nique
luh peek neek
picnic

la fête foraine
lah fet forain
fairground

la pêche
lah pesh
fishing

l'équitation
laykeetasyohn
horseback riding

le parc safari
luh park safaree
safari park

le parc d'attraction
luh park datraksyohn
amusement park

SPORTS AND LEISURE

France offers the traveler a wide range of cultural
events, entertainments, leisure activities, and sports.
The French are proud of their funding for the arts,
including music, opera, the theater, and film. Their heritage
and culture are very important, and many people take a
keen interest in the arts, philosophy, and politics. There is
also a wide range of sports facilities, from winter sports,
climbing, and hiking in the Alps to watersports around
the coast and on inland lakes.

LEISURE TIME

I like...	J'aime... *jaym*
...art and painting	...l'art et la peinture *lar ay lah pahntewr*
...movies	...le cinéma *luh seenayma*
...the theater	...le théâtre *luh tayahtr*
...opera	...l'opéra *lopaira*
I prefer...	Je préfère... *juh prayfair*
...reading books	...lire *leer*
...listening to music	...écouter de la musique *aykootay duh lah mewzeek*
...watching sports	...regarder le sport *ruhgarday luh spor*
...going to concerts	...aller à des concerts *allay ah day kohnsair*
...dancing	...danser *dohnsay*
...going to clubs	...sortir en boîte *sorteer ohn bwat*
...going out with friends	...sortir avec des amis *sorteer avek dayzamee*
I don't like...	Je n'aime pas... *juh naym pah*
That doesn't interest me	Ça ne m'intéresse pas *sah nuh mahntairess pah*

AT THE BEACH

Can I rent...	Je peux louer... *juh puh looay*
...a jet-ski?	...un jet ski? *uhn jet skee*
...a beach umbrella?	...un parasol? *uhn parasol*
...a surfboard?	...une planche de surf? *ewn plohnsh duh surf*
...a wetsuit?	...une combinaison? *ewn kohnbeenayzohn*

la serviette
de plage
*lah sairvyet
duh plaj*
beach towel

le transat
luh trohnzat
deck chair

le ballon
de plage
*luh balohn
duh plaj*
beach ball

la chaise
longue
*lah shayz
lohng*
lounge chair

YOU MAY SEE...

Baignade interdite
baynyad ahntairdeet
No swimming

Plage fermée
plaj fairmay
Beach closed

Courants violents
koorohn vyolohn
Strong currents

How much does it cost?	Ça coûte combien? *sah koot kohnbyahn*
Can I go water-skiing?	Je peux faire du ski nautique? *juh puh fair dew skee noteek*
Is there a lifeguard?	Il y a un sauveteur? *eeleaya uhn sovtuhr*
Is it safe to...	C'est dangereux de... *say dohnjuhruh duh*
...swim here?	...nager ici? *najay eesee*
...surf here?	...faire du surf ici? *fair dew surf eesee*

les lunettes de soleil
lay lewnet duh solay
sunglasses

le chapeau (de soleil)
luh shapo duh sohlay
sun hat

les palmes
lay palm
fins

la crème solaire
lah kraym solair
suntan lotion

le maillot
luh mahyo
bikini

le masque et le tuba
luh mask ay luh tewbah
mask and snorkel

AT THE SWIMMING POOL

What time... À quelle heure...
ah kayl uhr

...does the pool open? ...ouvre la piscine?
oovruh lah peeseen

...does the pool close? ...ferme la piscine?
fairm lah peeseen

Is it... C'est...
say

...an indoor pool? ...une piscine couverte?
ewn peeseen koovairt

...an outdoor pool? ...une piscine découverte?
ewn peeseen daykoovairt

Is there a children's pool? Il y a un bassin pour les enfants?
eeleeya uhn basahn poor layzohnfohn

Where are the changing rooms? Où sont les vestiaires?
oo sohn lay vaystyair

Is it safe to dive? On peut plonger?
ohn puh plohnjay

le brassard
luh brassar
water wings

la planche
lah plohnsh
float

les lunettes
lay lewnet
swimming goggles

le maillot de bain
luh mahyo duh bahn
swimsuit

AT THE GYM

le cross trainer
luh kross trainuhr
cross trainer

le vélo d'exercice
luh stepuhr
exercise bike

le rameur
luh rahmuhr
rowing machine

le stepper
luh stepuhr
step machine

Is there a gym?	Il y a une salle de gym? *eeleeya ewn sahl duh jeem*
Is it free for guests?	C'est gratuit pour les clients? *say gratwee poor lay kliyohn*
Do I have to wear sneakers?	Il faut porter des tennis? *eel foh portay day taynis*
Do I need an introductory session?	Il faut suivre une séance de présentation? *eel foh sweevr ewn sayohns duh prayzohntasyohn*
Do you hold...	Vous proposez... *voo propozay*
...aerobics classes?	...des cours d'aérobic? *day koor da-airohbeek*
...Pilates classes?	...des cours de pilates? *day koor duh peelates*
...yoga classes?	...des cours de yoga? *day koor duh yoga*

BOATING AND SAILING

Can I rent...	Je peux louer... *juh puh looay*
...a dinghy?	...un canot pneumatique? *uhn kanoh pnuhmahteek*
...a windsurf board?	...une planche à voile? *ewn plohnsh ah vwal*
...a canoe?	...un canoë? *uhn kanoay*
...a rowboat?	...une barque *ewn bark*
Do you offer sailing lessons?	Vous proposez des cours de voile? *voo propozay day koor duh vwal*
Do you have a mooring?	Vous avez un bassin d'amarrage? *voo zavay uhn basahn dahmaraj*
How much is it for the night?	C'est combien pour la nuit? *say kohnbyahn poor lah nwee*
Can I buy gas?	On peut acheter de l'essence? *ohn puh ashuhtay duh laysohns*
Where is the marina?	Où se trouve le port de plaisance? *oo suh troov luh por duh playzohns*
Can you repair it?	Vous pouvez le réparer? *voo poovay luh raypahray*
I would like to rent...	Je voudrais louer... *juh voodray looay*

un gilet de sauvetage
uhn jeelay duh sovtaj
life jacket

une boussole
ewn boosol
compass

WINTER SPORTS

...some skis	...des skis *day skee*
...some ski boots	...des chaussures de ski *day shosewr duh skee*
...some poles	...des bâtons *day batohn*
...a snowboard	...une planche de snowboard *ewn plohnsh duh snowbord*
...a helmet	...un casque *uhn kask*
When does...	À quelle heure... *ah kayl uhr*
...the chair lift start?	...démarre le télésiège? *daymahr luh taylaysyayj*
...the cable car finish?	...ferme le téléphérique? *fairm luh taylayfaireek*
How much is a lift pass?	C'est combien pour le forfait? *say kohnbyahn poor luh fohrfay*
Can I take skiing lessons?	Vous donnez des cours de ski? *voo donay day koor duh skee*
Where are the green slopes?	Où sont les pistes vertes? *oo sohn lay peest vairt*

YOU MAY HEAR...

Vous êtes débutant?
voo zayt daybewtohn
Are you a beginner?

Je dois prendre une caution
juh dwa prohndr ewn kohsyohn
I need a deposit

BALL GAMES

I like playing...	J'aime jouer au... *jaym jooey oh*
...soccer	...football *football*
...tennis	...tennis *taynees*
...golf	...golf *golf*
...badminton	...badminton *badminton*
...squash	...squash *skwash*
...baseball	...baseball *baseball*
Where is...	Où se trouve... *oo suh troov*
...the tennis court?	...le court de tennis? *luh koor duh taynees*
...the golf course?	...le terrain de golf? *luh tairahn duh golf*
...the sports center?	...le complexe sportif? *luh kohnplayx sporteef*

le ballon
de football
*luh balohn
duh football*
soccer ball

le panier de basket
luh panyay duh basket
basket

le gant de baseball
luh gohn duh baseball
baseball glove

May I book a court...	Je peux louer un court... *juh puh looay uhn koor*
...for two hours?	...pour deux heures? *poor duh zuhr*
...at three o'clock?	...à trois heures? *ah trwa zuhr*
What shoes are allowed?	Faut-il des chaussures spéciales? *fohteel day shosewr spaysyahl*
May I rent...	Je peux louer... *juh puh looay*
...a tennis racket?	...une raquette de tennis? *ewn rahket duh taynees*
...some balls?	...des balles? *day bahl*
...a set of clubs?	...des clubs? *day club*
When is the game/ match?	À quelle heure est la partie/le match? *ah kayl uhr ay lah partee/ luh match*

le club de golf
luh club duh golf
golf club

les balles
de tennis
*lay bahl
duh taynees*
tennis balls

les poignets éponge
lay pwannay aypohnj
wristbands

la balle de golf, le té de golf
lah bahl duh golf luh tay duh golf
golf ball and tee

la raquette de tennis
lah rahket duh taynees
tennis racket

SPORTS AND LEISURE

GOING OUT

Where is...	Où se trouve... *oo suh troov*
...the opera house?	...l'opéra? *lopairah*
...the jazz club?	...le club de jazz? *luh klub duh jazz*
Do I have to book in advance?	Il faut réserver à l'avance? *eel foh rayzairvay ah lahvohns*
I'd like...tickets	Je voudrais...billets *juh voodray...beeyay*
I'd like seats...	Je voudrais des places... *juh voodray day plass*
...at the back	...à l'arrière *ah lahryair*
...at the front	...devant *duhvohn*
...in the middle	...au milieu *oh meelyuh*
...in the balcony	...au balcon *oh bahlkohn*
Is there live music?	Il y a un orchestre? *eeleeya uhn ohrkaystruh*
Can we go dancing?	On peut aller danser? *ohn puh allay dohnsay*

YOU MAY HEAR...

Veuillez éteindre
votre portable
*vuhvay aytahndr
votr portahbl*
**Turn off your cell
phone**

Veuillez retourner
à vos places
*vuhvay ruhtoornay
ah vo plass*
Return to your seats

le musicien
luh mewzeesyahn
musician

le théâtre
luh tayahtr
theater

l'opéra
lopairah
opera house

la boîte de nuit
lah bwat duh nwee
nightclub

le chanteur
luh shohntuhr
singer

la pianiste
lah pyaneest
pianist

le cinéma
luh seenaymah
movie theater

le pop-corn
lay popkorn
popcorn

le casino
luh kahzeeno
casino

la danse classique
lah dohns klasik
ballet

GALLERIES AND MUSEUMS

What are the opening hours?	Quels sont les horaires d'ouverture? *kayl sohn lay zohrair doovairtewr*
Are there guided tours in English?	Il y a des visites guidées en anglais? *eeleeya day veezeet geeday ohn ohnglay*
When does the tour leave?	À quelle heure commence la visite? *ah kayl uhr komohns lah veezeet*
How much does it cost?	C'est combien? *say kohnbyahn*
How long does it take?	Ça prend combien de temps? *sah prohn kohnbyahn duh tohn*
Do you have an audio guide?	Vous avez un guide audio? *voo zavay uhn geed audio*
Do you have a guidebook in English?	Vous avez un guide en anglais? *voo zavay uhn geed ohn ohnglay*
Is (flash) photography allowed?	On peut prendre des photos (au flash)? *ohn puh prohndr day foto oh flash*
Can you direct me to...?	Vous pouvez m'indiquer...? *voo poovay mahndeekay*
I'd really like to see...	J'aimerais beaucoup voir... *jaymuhray bohkoo vwar*

la statue
lah stahtew
statue

le buste
luh bewst
bust

Who painted this?	Qui a peint ça? *kee ah puhn sah*
How old is it?	De quand date-t-il? *duh kohn daht teel*
Are there wheelchair ramps?	Il y a un accès pour les fauteuils roulants? *eeleeya uhn nahksay poor lay fohtuhy roolohn*
Is there an elevator	Il y a un ascenseur? *eeleeya uhn nahsohnsuhr*
Where are the restrooms?	Où sont les toilettes? *oo sohn lay twalet*
I'm with a group	Je fais partie d'un groupe *juh fay partee duhn groop*
I've lost my group	J'ai perdu mon groupe *jay pairdew mohn groop*

le tableau
luh tabloh
painting

le dessin
luh daysahn
drawing

la gravure
lah gravewr
engraving

le manuscrit
luh manewskree
manuscript

HOME ENTERTAINMENT

How do I...	Comment fait-on pour... *komohn faytohn poor*
...turn on the television?	...allumer la télévision? *ahlewmay lah taylayveezyohn*
...change channels?	...changer de chaîne? *shohnjay duh shayn*
...turn up the volume?	...monter le son? *mohntay luh sohn*
...turn down the volume?	...baisser le son? *baysay luh sohn*
Do you have satellite TV?	Vous avez la télé satellite? *voo zavay lah taylay sahtayleet*
Where can I buy...	Où peut-on acheter... *oo puh tohn ashuhtay*
...a DVD?	...un DVD? *uhn dayvayday*
...a music CD?	...un CD de musique? *uhn sayday duh mewzeek*
...an audio CD?	...un CD audio? *uhn sayday audio*

le lecteur de DVD
luh layktuhr duh dayvayday
DVD player

le téléviseur grand écran
luh taylayveezuhr grohn taykrohn
widescreen TV

la télécommande
lah taylaykomohnd
remote control

la console de jeux
lah kohnsol duh juh
video game

la clé USB
lah klay ewaysbay
USB flash drive

l'ordinateur portable
lordeenatuhr portahbl
laptop

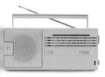

la radio
lah rahdio
radio

le disque dur
luh disk dewr
hard drive

la souris
lah sooree
mouse

Can I use this to...	Je peux l'utiliser pour... *juh puh lewteeleezay poor*
...go online?	...aller sur internet? *allay sewr ahntairnet*
Do you have broadband/wifi?	Vous avez l'ADSL?/le wifi? *voo zavay layl/weefee*
How do I...	Que faut-il faire pour... *kuh foh teel fair poor*
...log on?	...se connecter? *suh konayktay*
...log out?	...se déconnecter? *suh daykonayktay*
...reboot?	...redémarrer? *ruhdaymahray*

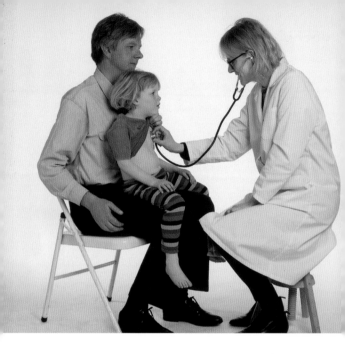

HEALTH

EU nationals receive free emergency medical care in France, provided they produce a European Health Insurance Card. Visitors from outside the EU should ensure that their health insurance covers them for medical treatment in France, or purchase special travel insurance. It is a good idea to familiarize yourself with a few basic phrases in case you need to visit a pharmacy or doctor.

USEFUL PHRASES

I need a doctor	Il faut que je voie un médecin *eel foh kuh juh vwa uhn mayduhsahn*
I would like an appointment...	Je voudrais prendre un rendez-vous... *juh voodray prohndr uhn rohnday voo*
...as soon as possible	...dès que possible *day kuh pohseebl*
...today	...aujourd'hui *oh-joordwee*
It's very urgent	C'est très urgent *say tray zewrjohn*
I have a European Health Insurance Card	J'ai une carte européenne d'assurance maladie *jay ewn kart uhropayen dassewrohns maladee*
I have health insurance	J'ai une assurance maladie *jay ewn assewrohns maladee*
May I have a receipt?	Je peux avoir un reçu? *juh puh avwar uhn ruhsew*
Where is the nearest...?	Où se trouve...la/le plus proche? *oo suh troov lah/luh plew prohsh*
...pharmacy...	...pharmacie... *farmasee*
...doctor's office...	...cabinet médical... *kahbeenay maydeekal*
...hospital...	...hôpital... *opeetal*
...dentist...	...dentiste... *dohnteest*
What are the opening times?	Quels sont les horaires d'ouverture? *kayl sohn lay zohrair doovairtewr*

AT THE PHARMACY

What can I take for...?	Qu'est-ce-que je peux prendre pour...? *keskuh juh puh prohndr poor*
How much should I take?	Il faut en prendre combien? *eel foh ohn prohndr kohnbyahn*
Is it safe for children?	Les enfants peuvent en prendre? *lay zohnfohn puhv tohn prohndr*
Are there side effects?	Il y a des effets secondaires? *eeleeya day zayfay suhgohndair*
Do you have that...	Vous en avez... *voo zohn navay*
...in tablet form?	...en cachets? *ohn kahshay*
...as a spray?	...en vaporisateur? *ohn vapohreezahtuhr*
...in capsule form?	...en capsules? *ohn kapsewl*
I'm allergic to...	Je suis allergique au/à la... *juh swee ahlairjeek oh/ah lah*
I'm already taking...	Je prends déjà... *juh prohn dayjah*
Do I need a prescription?	Il me faut une ordonnance? *eel muh foh ewn ordonohns*

YOU MAY HEAR...

C'est à prendre...fois par jour
say tah prohndr...fwa par joor
Take this...times a day

Pendant les repas
pohndohn lay ruhpah
With food

le bandage
luh bohndaj
bandage

les pansements
lay pohnsmohn
adhesive bandage

les capsules
lay kapsewl
capsules

les cachets
lay kashay
pills

la pommade
lah pomad
ointment

les suppositoires
lay sewpozeetwar
suppositories

les gouttes
lay goot
drops

l'inhalateur
leenahlahtuhr
inhaler

le vaporisateur
luh vapohreezahtuhr
spray

le sirop
luh seeroh
syrup

THE HUMAN BODY

I have hurt my... Je me suis fait mal au/à la...
juh muh swee fay mal oh/ah lah

I have cut my... Je me suis coupé le/la...
juh muh swee koopay luh/lah

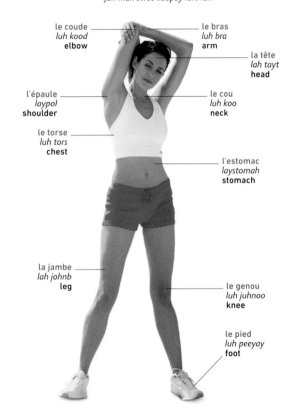

le coude
luh kood
elbow

le bras
luh bra
arm

la tête
lah tayt
head

l'épaule
laypol
shoulder

le cou
luh koo
neck

le torse
luh tors
chest

l'estomac
laystomah
stomach

la jambe
lah johnb
leg

le genou
luh juhnoo
knee

le pied
luh peeyay
foot

FACE

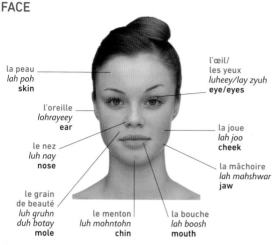

la peau
lah poh
skin

l'œil/
les yeux
luheey/lay zyuh
eye/eyes

l'oreille
lohrayeey
ear

la joue
lah joo
cheek

le nez
luh nay
nose

la mâchoire
lah mahshwar
jaw

le grain
de beauté
*luh gruhn
duh botay*
mole

le menton
luh mohntohn
chin

la bouche
lah boosh
mouth

HAND   ## FOOT

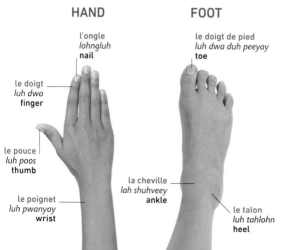

l'ongle
lohngluh
nail

le doigt de pied
luh dwa duh peeyay
toe

le doigt
luh dwa
finger

le pouce
luh poos
thumb

la cheville
lah shuhveey
ankle

le poignet
luh pwanyay
wrist

le talon
luh tahlohn
heel

FEELING SICK

I don't feel well	Je ne me sens pas bien *juh nuh muh sohn pah byahn*
I feel sick	Je me sens malade *juh muh sohn malad*
I have...	J'ai... *jay*
...an ear ache	...mal à l'oreille *mal ah lohrayeey*
...a stomach ache	...mal au ventre *mal oh vohntr*
...a sore throat	...mal à la gorge *mal ahla gohrj*
...a temperature	...de la fièvre *duh lah fyayvr*
...hayfever	...le rhume des foins *luh rewm day fwahn*
...diarrhea	...la diarrhée *lah dyahray*
...toothache	...mal aux dents *mal oh dohn*
I have constipation	Je suis constipé/constipée *juh swee kohnsteepay*
I've been stung/bitten by...	Je me suis fait piquer par... *juh muh swee fay peekay par*
...a bee/wasp	...une abeille/une guêpe *ewn ahbayeey/ewn gayp*
...a jellyfish	...une méduse *ewn maydewz*
...a snake	...un serpent *uhn sairpohn*
I've been bitten by a dog	Je me suis fait mordre par un chien *juh muh swee fay mohrdr par uhn shyahn*

INJURIES

une morsure
ewn morsewr
bite

une piqûre
ewn peekewr
sting

une fracture
ewn fraktewr
fracture

une égratignure
ewn aygrahteenyewr
graze

une écharde
ewn ayshard
splinter

une brûlure
ewn brewlewr
burn

une coupure
ewn koopewr
cut

un bleu
uhn bluh
bruise

un coup de soleil
uhn koo duh solayeey
sunburn

une foulure
ewn foolewr
sprain

AT THE DOCTOR

I need to see a doctor	Il faut que je voie un médecin *eel foh kuh juh vwa uhn mayduhsahn*
I'm...	Je... *juh*
...vomiting	...vomis *vohmee*
...bleeding	...saigne *saynyuh*
...feeling faint	...me sens faible *muh sohn faybl*
I'm pregnant	Je suis enceinte *juh swee ohnsahnt*
I'm diabetic	Je suis diabétique *juh swee dyahbayteek*
I'm epileptic	Je suis épileptique *juh swee aypeelaypteek*
I have...	J'ai... *jay*
...arthritis	...de l'arthrite *duh lartreet*
...a heart condition	...un problème cardiaque *uhn problem kahrdyak*
...high blood pressure	...de la tension artérielle *duh lah tohnsyohn artairyayl*

YOU MAY HEAR...

Qu'est-ce qui ne
va pas?
kes kee nuh vah pah
What's wrong?

Où avez-vous mal?
oo avay voo mal
**Where does
it hurt?**

Je peux vous examiner?
juh puh voo zayxameenay
May I examine you?

ILLNESS

la toux
lah too
cough

l'asthme
lassm
asthma

le rhume
luh rewm
cold

la grippe
lah greep
the flu

l'éternuement
laytairnewmohn
sneeze

le mal au ventre
luh mal oh vohntr
stomach cramps

la nausée
lah nohzay
nausea

les plaques rouges
lay plak rooj
rash

le saignement de nez
luh saynyuhmohn duh nay
nosebleed

le mal de tête
luh mal duh tet
headache

AT THE HOSPITAL

Can you help me?	Vous pouvez m'aider? *voo poovay mayday*
I need...	Je voudrais voir... *juh voodray vwar*
...a doctor	...un médecin *uhn mayduhsahn*
...a nurse	...une infirmière *ewn ahnfeermyair*
Where is/are...	Où se trouve/trouvent... *oo se troov/troov*
...the emergency room?	...les urgences? *lay zewrjohns*
...the children's ward?	...le service de pédiatrie? *luh sairvees duh paydyahtree*
...the X-ray department?	...le service de radiologie? *luh sairvees duh rahdyolojee*
...the waiting room?	...la salle d'attente? *lah sahl dahtohnt*

une piqûre
ewn peekewr
injection

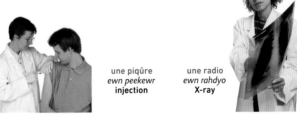

une radio
ewn rahdyo
X-ray

un prélèvement
de sang
*uhn praylayvmohn
duh sohn*
blood test

un scanner
uhn skanair
scan

...the intensive care unit?	...les soins intensifs? *lay swahn ahntohnseef*
...the elevator/stairs?	...l'ascenseur/les escaliers? *lasohnsuhr/lay zayskahlyay*
I've broken...	Je me suis cassé... *juh muh swee kahsay*
Do I need...	Il me faut... *eel muh foh*
...an injection?	...une piqûre? *ewn peekewr*
...antibiotics?	...des antibiotiques? *day zohnteebyohteek*
...an operation?	...subir une opération? *sewbeer ewn ohpairahsyohn*
Will it hurt?	Ça va faire mal? *sah vah fair mal*
What are the visiting hours?	Quels sont les horaires de visite? *kel sohn lay zohrair duh veezeet*

le bouche-à-bouche
luh boosh ah boosh
resuscitation

un fauteuil roulant
uhn fotuhy roolohn
wheelchair

une attelle
ewn atel
splint

un bandage
uhn bohndaj
dressing

EMERGENCIES

In an emergency, you should dial 15 to call an ambulance (*ambulance*), 18 for the fire department (*les pompiers*), or 17 to contact the police (called *la police* in cities and major towns, but *la gendarmerie* in smaller towns and villages). The pan-European emergency number is 112. If you are the victim of a crime or you lose your passport and money, you should report the incident to the police.

Help!	À l'aide! *ah layd*
Please go away!	Laissez-moi tranquille! *layssay mwa trohnkeel*
Let go!	Lâchez-moi! *lashay mwa*
Stop! Thief!	Arrêtez! Au voleur! *araytay oh vohluhr*
Call the police!	Appelez la police! *apuhlay lah polees*
Get a doctor!	Appelez un médecin! *apuhlay uhn mayduhsahn*
I need...	Il me faut... *eel muh foh*
...the police	...la police *lah pohlees*
...the fire department	...les pompiers *lay pohnpyay*
...an ambulance	...une ambulance *ewn ohnbewlohns*
It's very urgent	C'est très urgent *say tray zewrjohn*
Where is...	Où se trouve... *oo suh troov*
...the American/British embassy?	...l'ambassade des États-Unis/du Royaume-Uni? *lohnbahsahd day zaytah zewnee/ dewrwahyohm ewnee*
...the police station?	...le commissariat? *luh komeesaryah*
...the hospital?	...l'hôpital? *lopeetal*

ACCIDENTS

I need to make a telephone call	Il faut que je passe un coup de fil *eel foh kuh juh pass uhn koo duh feel*
I'd like to report an accident	Je voudrais faire une déclaration d'accident *juh voodray fair ewn dayklarasyohn dakseedohn*
I've crashed my car	J'ai eu un accident *jay ew uhn akseedohn*
The registration number is...	La plaque d'immatriculation est... *lah plak deematreekewlahsyon ay*
I'm at...	Je suis à... *juh sweezah*
Please come quickly!	Venez vite, s'il vous plaît! *vuhnay veet seel voo play*
Someone's injured	Il y a un blessé *eeleeya uhn blayssay*
Someone's been knocked down	Quelqu'un s'est fait renverser *kelkuhn say fay rohnvairsay*
There's a fire at...	Il y a un incendie à... *eeleeya uhn ahnsohndee ah*
Someone is trapped in the building	Quelqu'un est bloqué dans le bâtiment *kelkuhn ay blohkay dohn luh bateemohn*

YOU MAY HEAR...

Quel service désirez-vous?
kel servees dayzeeray voo
Which service do you require?

Que s'est-il passé?
kuh say teel passay
What happened?

EMERGENCY SERVICES

la bouche d'incendie
lah boosh dahnsohndee
fire hydrant

les pompiers
lay pohnpyay
firefighters

l'extincteur
lextahnktuhr
fire extinguisher

la voiture de police
lah vwatewr duh polees
police car

les menottes
lay muhnot
handcuffs

l'alarme incendie
lalarm ahnsohndee
fire alarm

le policier
luh poleesyay
police officer

l'ambulance
lohnbewlohns
ambulance

le camion
de pompiers
*luh kamyohn
duh pohnpyay*
fire engine

POLICE AND CRIME

I want to report a crime	Je voudrais signaler un délit *juh voodray seenyalay uhn daylee*
I've been robbed	On m'a volé mes affaires *ohn mah volay may zahfair*
I've been attacked	Je me suis fait attaquer *juh muh swee fay atahkay*
I've been mugged	Je me suis fait agresser *juh muh swee fay agresay*
I've been raped	Je me suis fait violer *juh muh swee fay vyohlay*
I've been burgled	Je me suis fait cambrioler *juh muh swee fay kohnbreeyolay*
Someone has stolen...	On m'a volé... *ohn mah volay*
...my car	...ma voiture *mah vwatewr*
...my money	...mon argent *mohn narjohn*
...my bag	...mon sac *mohn sak*
...my passport	...mon passeport *mohn passpor*

YOU MAY HEAR...

C'est arrivé quand?
say tareevay kohn
When did it happen?

Il était comment?
eel aytay kohmohn
What did he look like?

Il y a des témoins?
eeleeya day taymwuhn
Was there a witness?

I'd like to speak to...	Je voudrais parler à... *juh voodray parlay ah*
...a senior officer	...un inspecteur *uhn ahnspayktuhr*
...a policewoman	...une femme policier *uhn fahm poleesyay*
I need...	Je voudrais... *juh voodray*
...a lawyer	...un avocat *uhn navohkah*
...an interpreter	...un interprète *uhn ahntayrprayt*
...to make a phone call	...passer un coup de fil *passay uhn koo duh feel*
Here is...	Voici... *vwassee*
...my driver's license	...mon permis de conduire *mohn pairmee duh kohndweer*
...my insurance	...mes papiers d'assurance *may papyay dasewrohns*
How much is the fine?	À combien est l'amende? *Ah kohnbyahn ay lahmohnd*
Where do I pay it?	Où faut-il payer? *oo foh teel payay*

YOU MAY HEAR...

Votre permis, s'il vous plaît
votruh pairmee seel voo play
Your license please

Vos papiers, s'il vous plaît
voh papyay seel voo play
Your papers please

AT THE GARAGE

Where is the nearest garage?	Où se trouve le garage le plus proche? *oo suh troov luh garaj luh plew prosh*
Can you do repairs?	Vous faites les réparations? *voo fayt lay rayparasyohn*
I need...	Il me faut... *eel muh foh*
...a new tire	...un nouveau pneu *uhn noovoh pnuh*
...a new exhaust	...un nouveau pot d'échappement *uhn noovoh poh dayshapmohn*
...a new windshield	...un nouveau pare-brise *uhn noovoh par breez*
...a new headlight	...une nouvelle ampoule *ewn noovel ohnpool*
...new wiper blades	...de nouveaux essuie-glaces *de noovoh zayswee glass*
Do you have one?	Vous en avez? *voo zohn nahvay*
Can you replace this?	Vous pouvez le remplacer? *voo poovay luh rohnplassay*
The...is not working	Le/la...ne fonctionne pas *luh/lah...nuh fohnksyon pah*
There is something wrong with the engine	Il y a un problème au niveau du moteur *eeleeya uhn problaym oh neevo dew motuhr*
Is it serious?	C'est grave? *say grav*
When will it be ready?	Ça sera prêt quand? *sah suhrah pray kohn*
How much will it cost?	Ça va coûter combien? *sah vah kootay kohnbyahn*

CAR BREAKDOWN

My car has broken down
Ma voiture est en panne
mah vwatewr ayt ohn pahnn

Can you help me?
Vous pouvez m'aider?
voo poovay mayday

Please come to...
Vous pouvez venir à...
voo poovay vuhneer ah

I have a flat tire
J'ai un pneu crevé
jay uhn pnuh kruhvay

Can you change the wheel?
Vous pouvez changer la roue?
voo poovay shohnjay lah roo

My car won't start
Ma voiture ne démarre pas
mah vwatewr nuh daymar pah

The engine is overheating
Le moteur surchauffe
luh mohtuhr sewrshof

Can you fix it?
Vous pouvez le réparer?
voo poovay luh rayparay

I've run out of gasoline
Je n'ai plus d'essence
juh nay plew daysohns

Can you tow me to a garage?
Vous pouvez me remorquer jusqu'au garage?
voo poovay muh ruhmohrkay jewskoh garaj

YOU MAY HEAR...

Qu'est-ce qui ne va pas?
keskee nuh vah pah
What is the problem?

Vous avez une roue de secours?
voo zavay ewn roo duh suhkoor
Do you have a spare tire?

LOST PROPERTY

I've lost...	J'ai perdu... *jay pairdew*
...my money	...mon argent *mohn nahrjohn*
...my keys	...mes clés *may klay*
...my glasses	...mes lunettes *may lewnet*
My luggage is missing	Mes bagages ont disparu *may bagaj ohn deesparew*
My suitcase has been damaged	Ma valise a été endommagée *mah valees ah aytay ohndomajay*

le portefeuille
luh portuhfuhy
wallet

le passeport
luh passpor
passport

la carte de crédit
lah kart duh kraydee
credit card

le porte-monnaie
luh port mohnay
change purse

l'appareil photo
laparayeey foto
camera

le smartphone
luh smartfohn
smartphone

la serviette
lah sayrveeyet
briefcase

le sac à main
luh sak ah mahn
handbag

la valise
lah valeez
suitcase

I need to phone my insurance company	Il faut que je téléphone à mon assurance *eel foh kuh juh taylayfon ah mohn nassewrohns*
Can I put a stop on my credit cards?	Je peux bloquer mes cartes de crédit? *juh puh blokay may kart duh kraydee*
My name is...	Je m'appelle... *juh mapel*
My policy number is...	Mon numéro d'adhérent est le... *mohn newmairo dadairohn ay luh*
My address is...	Mon adresse est... *mohn nadress ay*
My contact number is...	Mon numéro de téléphone est le... *mohn newmairo duh taylayfohn ay luh*
My email address is...	Mon adresse e-mail est... *mohn nadress email ay*

MENU GUIDE

This guide lists the most common terms you may come across on French menus or when shopping for food. If you can't find an exact phrase, try looking up its component parts.

A

abats *offal*
abricot *apricot*
à emporter *to carry out*
agneau *lamb*
aiguillette de bœuf
  slices of rump steak
ail *garlic*
aïoli *garlic mayonnaise*
à l'ancienne *traditional style*
à la broche *spit roast*
à la boulangère *baked in the oven with sliced potatoes and onions*
à la jardinière *with assorted vegetables*
à la lyonnaise *garnished with onions*
à la marinière *cooked in white wine*
à la normande *in cream sauce*
à la vapeur *steamed*
amande *almond*
amuse-bouche *appetizer*
ananas *pineapple*
anchoïade *anchovy and tomato paste*
anchois *anchovies*
andouillette *spicy sausage*
anguille *eel*
à point *medium (steak)*
artichaut *artichoke*
asperge *asparagus*

assiette anglaise *selection of cold meats*
au gratin *baked in a cheese sauce*
au vin blanc *in white wine*
avocat *avocado*

B

banane *banana*
barbue *brill (fish)*
basilic *basil*
bavaroise *light mousse*
béarnaise *with butter sauce*
bécasse *woodcock*
béchamel *white sauce*
beignet *fritter, doughnut*
betterave *beet*
beurre *butter*
beurre d'anchois *anchovy paste*
beurre noir *dark, melted butter*
bien cuit *well done*
bière *beer*
bière à la pression *draught beer*
bière blonde *lager*
bière brune *bitter beer*
bifteck *steak*
bisque *fish soup*
blanquette de veau *veal stew*
bleu *very rare steak*
Bleu d'Auvergne *blue cheese from Auvergne*
bœuf bourguignon *casserole of beef cooked in red wine*
bœuf braisé *braised beef*
bœuf en daube *beef casserole*

bœuf miroton *beef and onion stew*
bœuf mode *beef stew with carrots*
bolet *boletus (mushroom)*
bonne femme *traditional "home cooking" style*
bouchées *small puff pastries*
boudin blanc *white pudding*
boudin noir *black pudding*
bouillabaisse *fish soup*
bouilli *boiled*
bouillon *broth*
bouillon de légumes *vegetable stock*
bouillon de poule *chicken stock*
boulette *meatball*
bouquet rose *prawns*
bourride *fish soup*
brandade *cod in cream and garlic*
brioche *round roll containing egg and milk*
brochet *pike*
brochette *kebab*
brugnon *nectarine*
brûlot *flambéed brandy*
brut *very dry*

C

cabillaud *cod*
café *coffee (black)*
café au lait *coffee with milk*
café complet *continental breakfast*
café crème *coffee with cream*
café glacé *iced coffee*
café liégeois *iced coffee with cream*
caille *quail*
calamar/calmar *squid*
calvados *apple brandy*
canard *duck*
canard laqué *Peking duck*
caneton *duckling*

Cantal *white cheese from Auvergne*
câpres *capers*
carbonnade *beef cooked in beer*
cari *curry*
carotte *carrot*
carottes Vichy *carrots in butter and parsley*
carpe *carp*
carré d'agneau *rack of lamb*
carrelet *plaice*
carte *menu*
carte des vins *wine list*
casse-croûte *snacks*
cassis *blackcurrant*
cassoulet *bean, pork, and duck casserole*
céleri en branches *celery*
céleri rave *celeriac*
cèpe *cep (mushroom)*
cerise *cherry*
cerises à l'eau de vie *cherries in brandy*
cervelle *brains*
chabichou *goat's milk cheese*
Chablis *dry white wine from Burgundy*
champignon *mushroom*
champignon de Paris *white button mushroom*
chanterelle *chanterelle mushroom*
chantilly *whipped cream*
charcuterie *sausages, ham and pâtés; pork products*
charlotte *dessert with fruit, cream, and biscuits*
chasseur *with mushrooms and herbs*
chausson aux pommes *apple turnover*
cheval *horse*
chèvre *goat's cheese*
chevreuil *venison*
chicorée *endive*

chocolat chaud
hot chocolate
chocolat glacé
iced chocolate
chou *cabbage*
chou à la crème *cream puff*
choucroute *sauerkraut with sausages and ham*
chou-fleur *cauliflower*
chou rouge *red cabbage*
choux de Bruxelles
Brussels sprouts
cidre *cider*
citron *lemon*
citron pressé
fresh lemon juice
clafoutis *baked batter pudding with fruit*
cochon de lait *suckling pig*
cocotte, en cocotte *cooked in a casserole or ramekin*
coing *quince*
colin *hake*
compote *stewed fruit*
Comté *hard cheese from the Jura*
concombre *cucumber*
confit de canard *duck preserved in fat*
confit d'oie *goose preserved in fat*
confiture *jam*
congre *conger eel*
consommé *clear broth*
coq au vin *chicken in red wine*
coque *cockle*
coquilles Saint-Jacques
scallops in cream sauce
côte de porc *pork chop*
côtelette *chop*
cotriade bretonne *fish soup from Brittany*
coulis *sauce or purée*

Coulommiers *rich, soft cheese*
crabe *crab*
crème *cream; creamy sauce or dessert; white (coffee)*
crème à la vanille *vanilla custard*
crème anglaise *custard*
crème d'asperges *cream of asparagus soup*
crème de bolets *cream of mushroom soup*
crème de volaille *cream of chicken soup*
crème d'huîtres *cream of oyster soup*
crème pâtissière *rich, creamy custard*
crème renversée *set custard*
crème vichyssoise *chilled leek and potato soup*
crêpe de froment *wheat crêpe*
crêpes Suzette *crêpes flambéed with orange sauce*
crépinette *small sausage patty wrapped in fat*
cresson *cress*
crevette grise *shrimp*
crevette rose *prawn*
croque-madame *grilled cheese and ham sandwich with a fried egg*
croque-monsieur *grilled cheese and ham sandwich*
crottin de Chavignol *small goat's cheese*
crustacés *shellfish*
cuisses de grenouille
frogs' legs

D

dartois *pastry with jam*
daurade *sea bream*
dégustation *wine tasting*
digestif *liqueur*

dinde *turkey*
doux *sweet*

E

eau minérale gazeuse
sparkling mineral water
eau minérale plate *still*
mineral water
échalote *shallot*
écrevisse
freshwater crayfish
endive *chicory*
en papillote *baked in*
foil or paper
entrecôte *rib steak*
entrecôte maître d'hôtel *steak*
with butter and parsley
entrée *appetizer*
entremets *dessert*
épaule d'agneau farcie
stuffed shoulder of lamb
épinards *spinach*
escalope de veau milanaise
veal escalope with
tomato sauce
escalope panée
breaded escalope
escargot *snail*
estouffade de bœuf
beef casserole
estragon *tarragon*

F

faisan *pheasant*
farci *stuffed*
fenouil *fennel*
fève *fava bean*
filet *fillet*
filet de bœuf Rossini *fillet*
of beef with foie gras
filet de perche *perch fillet*
fine *brandy*
fines herbes *mixed herbs*

flageolets *flageolet beans*
flan *custard tart*
foie de veau *veal liver*
foie gras *goose or duck*
liver preserve
foies de volaille *chicken livers*
fonds d'artichaut *artichoke hearts*
fondue bourguignonne
meat fondue
fondue savoyarde *cheese fondue*
forestier *with mushrooms*
fraise *strawberry*
fraise des bois *wild strawberry*
framboise *raspberry*
frisée *curly lettuce*
frit *deep-fried*
frites *French fries*
fromage *cheese*
fromage blanc *fromage frais*
fromage de chèvre
goat's cheese
fruits de mer *seafood*
fumé *smoked*

G

galantine *rolled, stuffed*
meat or poultry
galette *round, flat cake or*
savoury wholemeal crèpe
garbure *thick soup*
garni *with potatoes*
and vegetables
gâteau *cake*
gaufre *wafer; waffle*
gelée *jelly*
Gewürztraminer *dry white*
wine from Alsace
gibier *game*
gigot d'agneau
leg of lamb
girolle *chanterelle mushroom*
glace *ice cream*
gougère *choux pastry dish*

goujon *gudgeon (fish)*
gratin *dish baked with cheese and cream*
gratin dauphinois *sliced potatoes baked in cream*
gratinée *baked onion soup*
grillé *broiled*
grondin *gurnard (fish)*
groseille rouge *red currant*

H

hachis parmentier *shepherd's pie*
hareng mariné *marinated herring*
haricots *beans*
haricots blancs *haricot beans*
haricots verts *green beans*
homard *lobster*
hors-d'œuvre *starter*
huître *oyster*

I

îles flottantes *soft meringues on custard*
infusion *herb tea*

J

jambon *ham*
jambon de Bayonne *smoked and cured ham*
julienne *soup with chopped vegetables*
jus de fruits *fruit juice*

K

kir *white wine with black currant liqueur*
kir royal *champagne with black currant liqueur*
kirsch *cherry brandy*

L

lait *milk*
laitue *lettuce*
langouste *spiny lobster*
langoustine *Dublin Bay shrimp/scampi*
lapereau *young rabbit*
lapin *rabbit*
lapin de garenne *wild rabbit*
lard *bacon*
lardon *small cube of bacon*
légume *vegetable*
lentilles *lentils*
lièvre *hare*
limande *lemon sole*
Livarot *strong, soft cheese*
lotte *monkfish*
loup de mer *sea bass*

M

macédoine de légumes *mixed vegetables*
mâche *lamb's lettuce*
maison *home-made*
mangue *mango*
maquereau *mackerel*
marc *grape brandy*
marcassin *young boar*
marchand de vin *in red wine sauce*
marjolaine *marjoram*
marron *chestnut*
massepain *marzipan*
menthe *peppermint*
menthe à l'eau *mint cordial with water*
menu du jour *today's menu*
menu gastronomique *gourmet menu*
menu touristique *tourist menu*
merlan *whiting*
mesclun *dark green leaf salad*
millefeuille *custard slice*

millésime *vintage*
morille *morel (mushroom)*
morue *cod*
moules *mussels*
moules marinière *mussels in white wine*
mousseline *fish mousse*
mousseux *sparkling*
moutarde *mustard*
mouton *mutton*
mulet *mullet*
Munster *strong cheese from eastern France*
mûre *blackberry*
muscade *nutmeg*
Muscadet *dry white wine*
myrtille *bilberry*

N

nature *plain*
navarin *mutton stew with vegetables*
navet *turnip*
noisette *hazelnut*
noisette d'agneau *medallion of lamb*
noix *nuts, walnuts*
nouilles *noodles*

O

œuf à la coque *boiled egg*
œuf dur *hard-boiled egg*
œuf mollet *soft-boiled egg*
œuf poché *poached egg*
œufs brouillés *scrambled eggs*
œuf sur le plat *fried egg*
oie *goose*
oignon *onion*
omelette au naturel *plain omelet*

omelette paysanne *omelet with potatoes and bacon*
orange pressée *fresh orange juice*
oseille *sorrel*
oursin *sea urchin*

P

pain *bread*
pain au chocolat *chocolate croissant*
pain complet *whole-wheat bread*
pain de seigle *rye bread*
palette de porc *shoulder of pork*
palourde *clam*
pamplemousse *grapefruit*
panaché *shandy*
pastis *anise-flavoured alcoholic drink*
pâte brisée *shortcrust pastry*
pâté de canard *duck pâté*
pâté de foie de volaille *chicken liver pâté*
pâte feuilletée *puff pastry*
pâtes *pasta*
pêche *peach*
perdreau *young partridge*
perdrix *partridge*
persillade *finely chopped parsley and garlic*
petite friture *whitebait*
petit pain *roll*
petit pois *peas*
petits fours *small pastries*
petit salé *salted pork*
petit suisse *fromage frais*
pied de porc *pig's feet*
pigeonneau *young pigeon*
pignatelle *cheese fritter*
pignon *pine nut*

pilaf de mouton *rice dish with mutton*
pintade *guinea fowl*
piperade *dish of egg, tomatoes, and peppers*
pissaladière provençale *dish similar to pizza but without tomatoes*
pissenlit *dandelion*
pistache *pistachio*
pistou *basil and garlic sauce*
plat du jour *dish of the day*
plateau de fromages *cheese board*
pochouse *fish casserole*
poire *pear*
poireau *leek*
pois chiches *chick peas*
poisson *fish*
poivre *pepper*
poivron *red/green pepper*
pomme *apple*
pomme de terre *potato*
pommes de terre à l'anglaise *boiled potatoes*
pommes de terre en robe de chambre/des champs *baked potatoes*
pommes de terre sautées *fried potatoes*
pommes frites *French fries*
pommes paille *thin fries*
pommes vapeur *steamed potatoes*
porc *pork*
potage *soup*
potage bilibi *fish and oyster soup*
potage Crécy *carrot and rice soup*
potage cressonnière *watercress soup*
potage Esaü *lentil soup*

potage parmentier *leek and potato soup*
potage printanier *vegetable soup*
potage Saint-Germain *split pea soup*
potage velouté *creamy soup*
potiron *pumpkin*
pot-au-feu *beef and vegetable stew*
potée *vegetable and meat stew*
Pouilly-Fuissé *dry white wine from Burgundy*
poule au pot *chicken and vegetable stew*
poulet basquaise *chicken with ratatouille*
poulet chasseur *chicken with mushrooms and white wine*
poulet créole *chicken in white sauce with rice*
poulet fermier *free-range chicken*
poulet rôti *roast chicken*
praire *clam*
printanier *with spring vegetables*
provençale *with tomatoes, garlic and herbs*
prune *plum*
pruneau *prune*
purée *mashed potatoes*

Q

quenelle *meat or fish dumpling*
queue de bœuf *oxtail*
quiche lorraine *egg, bacon, and cream tart*

R

raclette *Swiss dish of melted cheese*
radis *radish*
ragoût *stew*
raie *skate*

raie au beurre noir *skate fried in butter*

raifort *horseradish*

raisin *grape*

râpé *grated*

rascasse *scorpion fish*

ratatouille *stew of peppers, courgettes, eggplant, and tomatoes*

ravigote *herb dressing*

Reblochon *strong cheese from Savoy*

rémoulade *mayonnaise dressing with herbs, mustard, and capers*

Rigotte *small goat's cheese from Lyon*

rillettes *potted pork or goose meat*

ris de veau *veal sweetbread*

riz *rice*

riz pilaf *spicy rice with meat or seafood*

rognon *kidney*

Roquefort *blue cheese*

rôti *roasted/joint of meat*

rouget *mullet*

rouille *fish and chili sauce*

S

sabayon *zabaglione*

sablé *shortbread*

saignant *rare*

saint-honoré *cream puff cake*

Saint-marcellin *goat's cheese*

salade composée *mixed salad*

salade russe *diced vegetables in mayonnaise*

salade verte *green salad*

salmis *game stew*

salsifis *oyster plant, salsify*

sanglier *wild boar*

sauce aurore *white sauce with tomato purée*

sauce béarnaise *thick sauce of eggs and butter*

sauce blanche *white sauce*

sauce gribiche *dressing with hard-boiled eggs*

sauce hollandaise *rich sauce of eggs, butter, and vinegar*

sauce Madère *Madeira sauce*

sauce matelote *wine sauce*

sauce Mornay *béchamel sauce with cheese*

sauce mousseline *hollandaise sauce with cream*

sauce poulette *sauce of mushrooms and egg yolks*

sauce ravigote *dressing with shallots and herbs*

sauce suprême *creamy sauce*

sauce tartare *mayonnaise with herbs and gherkins*

sauce veloutée *white sauce with egg yolks and cream*

sauce vinot *wine sauce*

saucisse *sausage*

saucisse de Francfort *frankfurter*

saucisse de Strasbourg *beef sausage*

saucisson *salami*

sauge *sage*

saumon *salmon*

saumon fumé *smoked salmon*

Sauternes *sweet white wine*

savarin *rum baba*

sec *dry*

seiche *cuttlefish*

sel *salt*

service (non) compris *service (not) included*

sole bonne femme *sole in wine and mushrooms*
sole meunière *floured sole fried in butter*
soupe *soup*
soupe au pistou *thick vegetable soup with basil*
steak au poivre *peppered steak*
steak frites *steak and French fries*
steak haché *ground beef*
steak tartare *raw ground steak with a raw egg*
sucre *sugar*
suprême de volaille *chicken in cream sauce*

T

tanche *tench (fish)*
tapenade *Provencal olive and anchovy paste*
tarte *tart*
tarte frangipane *almond cream tart*
tartelette *small tart*
tarte Tatin *apple tart*
tartine *bread and butter*
tendrons de veau *breast of veal*
terrine *pâté*
tête de veau *calf's head*
thé *tea*
thé à la menthe *mint tea*
thé au lait *tea with milk*
thé citron *lemon tea*
tian *baked Provencal vegetable or fish dish*
thon *tuna*
tomates farcies *stuffed tomatoes*

tome de Savoie *white cheese from Savoy*
tournedos *round beef steak*
tourte *covered pie*
tourteau *type of crab*
tripes à la mode de Caen *tripe in spicy sauce*
truffe *truffle*
truite au bleu *poached trout*
truite aux amandes *trout with almonds*
truite meunière *trout in flour and fried in butter*

V

Vacherin *strong, soft cheese from the Jura*
vacherin glacé *ice cream meringue*
vanille *vanilla*
veau *veal*
velouté de tomate *cream of tomato soup*
vermicelle *vermicelli*
viande *meat*
vin *wine*
vinaigrette *French dressing*
vin blanc *white wine*
vin de pays *local wine*
vin de table *table wine*
vin rosé *rosé wine*
vin rouge *red wine*
volaille *poultry*
VSOP (Very Special Old Pale) *mature brandy*

Y

yaourt *yogurt*

DICTIONARY ENGLISH–FRENCH

The gender of a singular French noun is usually shown by the word for "the": *le* (masculine) or *la* (feminine). When *le* or *la* is abbreviated to *l'* before a vowel, the gender is shown by (**m**) or (**f**). After plural nouns following *les*, it is shown by (**m pl**) or (**f pl**). The singular masculine form of adjectives is given, followed by the singular feminine form.

A

a little *un peu*
a lot *beaucoup*
about *à propos de*
above *au-dessus de*
accident *l'accident* (m)
accident and emergency department *les urgences* (f pl)
accommodation *le logement*
account number *le numéro de compte*
across *à travers*
activities *les activités* (f pl)
actor *l'acteur* (m)
actress *l'actrice* (f)
adapter *l'adaptateur* (m)
add (verb) *additionner*
address *l'adresse* (f)
adhesive bandage *le pansement*
adhesive tape *le scotch*
adult *l'adulte* (m)
aerobics *l'aérobic* (f)
after *après*
afternoon *l'après-midi* (m)
aftersun *l'après-soleil* (m)
again *encore*
airbag *l'airbag* (m)
air-conditioning *la climatisation*
aircraft *l'avion* (m)
airmail *par avion*
airplane *l'avion* (m)
airport *l'aéroport* (m)

air travel *les voyages en avion* (m pl)
aisle *l'allée* (f)
aisle seat *la place couloir*
alarm clock *le réveil*
alcoholic drinks *les boissons alcoolisées* (f pl)
all *tout*
allergic *allergique*
allergy *l'allergie* (f)
almost *presque*
alone *seul/seule*
along *le long de*
already *déjà*
altitude *l'altitude* (f)
always *toujours*
ambulance *l'ambulance* (f)
amount *le montant*
amusement park *le parc d'attractions*
and *et*
angry *fâché/fâchée*
animals *les animaux* (m pl)
ankle *la cheville*
another *un autre/une autre*
answer (verb) *répondre*
answering machine *le répondeur*
antibiotics *les antibiotiques* (m pl)
antiseptic *l'antiseptique* (m)

apartment l'appartement (m)
apartment block l'immeuble (m)
appearance l'apparence (f)
appetizer l'entrée (f)
applaud (verb) applaudir
apple la pomme
apple juice le jus de pomme
application l'application (f)
appointment le rendez-vous
apricot l'abricot (m)
April avril
apron le tablier
arc l'arc (m)
arch la voûte
architect l'architecte (m/f)
architecture l'architecture (f)
area l'aire (f)
arm le bras
armband le brassard
around autour de
arrivals les arrivées (f pl)
arrive (verb) arriver
art l'art (m)
art gallery la galérie d'art
arthritis l'arthrite (f)
artificial sweetener
   l'édulcorant (m) artificiel
artist l'artiste peintre (m/f)
as comme
ashtray le cendrier
assistant l'assistant/
   l'assistante (m/f)
asthma l'asthme (m)
at à
athlete l'athlète (m/f)
ATM le distributeur
attachment la pièce jointe
attack l'attaque (f)
attend (verb) assister à
attractions les attractions (f pl)
audience le public
audio guide le guide audio
August août

aunt la tante
Australia l'Australie (f)
automatic automatique
automatic payment le prélèvement
automatic ticket machine
   le guichet automatique
avenue l'avenue (f)
avocado l'avocat (m)
awful horrible

B

baby le bébé
baby changing room
   la table à langer
babysitting la garde d'enfants
back le dossier
back (body) le dos
back (not front of) derrière
backpack le sac à dos
bacon le bacon
bad mauvais/mauvaise
badminton le badminton
bag le sac
bagel le bagel
baggage allowance la franchise
   de bagages
baggage claim le retrait
   des bagages
baguette la baguette
bake (verb) cuire au four
bakery la boulangerie
balcony le balcon
ball le ballon
ballet la danse classique
banana la banane
bandage le bandage
bank la banque
bank account le compte
   en banque
bank charge les frais
   bancaires (m pl)
bank manager le banquier
bank transfer le virement bancaire

bar *le bar*
bar snacks
 les amuse-gueules (m pl)
barbecue *le barbecue*
barber *le coiffeur*
bartender *le barman*
baseball *le baseball*
baseball mitt *le gant de baseball*
basement *le sous-sol*
basil *le basilic*
basket *le panier*
basketball *le basketball*
bath *le bain*
bathrobe *le peignoir*
bathroom *la salle de bain*
bath towel *la serviette de bain*
bathtub *la baignoire*
battery (car) *la batterie*
be (verb) *être*
beach *la plage*
beach ball *le ballon de plage*
beach towel *la serviette de plage*
beach umbrella *le parasol*
bear *l'ours (m)*
beautiful *beau/belle*
bed *le lit*
bed and breakfast (in hotel)
 la chambre avec petit déjeuner
bed and breakfast (guesthouse)
 la chambre d'hôte
bed linen *le linge de lit*
bedroom *la chambre*
bee *l'abeille (f)*
beef *le bœuf*
beer *la bière*
beet *la betterave*
beetle *le scarabée*
before *avant*
beginner *le débutant/la débutante*
beginning *le début*
behind *derrière*
bell *la sonnette*
below *en-dessous*

belt *la ceinture*
bench *le banc*
berry *la baie*
beside *à côté*
better *mieux*
between *entre*
beyond *au-delà de*
bicycle *le vélo*
bidet *le bidet*
big *grand/grande*
bike rack *le porte-vélos*
bikini *le maillot*
bill (note) *la note*
birds *les oiseaux (m pl)*
birth *la naissance*
birth certificate
 l'acte de naissance (m)
birthday *l'anniversaire (m)*
bit *le morceau*
bite (e.g. from an animal)
 la morsure
bitter *amer/amère*
black *noir/noire*
blackberry *la mûre*
blackcurrant *le cassis*
black coffee *le café (noir)*
black tea *le thé noir*
blanket *la couverture*
bleach *l'eau de Javel (f)*
bleeding *le saignement*
blender *le mixeur*
blister *l'ampoule (f)*
block *le blocage*
blonde *blond/blonde*
blood *le sang*
blood pressure
 la pression artérielle
blood test *l'analyse*
 de sang (f)
blouse *le chemisier*
blow dry (verb) *sécher*
blow-dryer *le sèche-cheveux*
blue *bleu/bleue*

blueberry *la myrtille*
blush *le fard à joues*
board (verb) *embarquer*
board, on *à bord*
boarding gate *la porte d'embarquement*
boarding pass *la carte d'embarquement*
boat *le bateau*
body *le corps*
body lotion *le lait corporel*
boil (verb) *bouillir*
book *le livre*
book (verb) *réserver*
book a flight (verb) *faire une réservation de vol*
bookstore *la librairie*
boot (footwear) *la botte*
bored, to be *s'ennuyer*
borrow (verb) *emprunter*
bottle *la bouteille*
bottle opener *l'ouvre-bouteille (m)*
bottled water *l'eau en bouteille (f)*
bowl *le bol*
bowling *le bowling*
box *la boîte*
box office *la caisse*
boy *le garçon*
boyfriend *le copain*
bracelet *le bracelet*
brain *le cerveau*
brake *le frein*
branch *la branche*
bread *le pain*
breakdown *la panne*
breakfast *le petit-déjeuner*
breakfast cereals *les céréales (f pl)*
brick *la brique*
bridge *le pont*
briefcase *la mallette*

briefs *le slip*
brioche *la brioche*
British *britannique*
broccoli *le brocoli*
broil (verb) *griller*
broken *cassé/cassée*
broom *le balai*
brother *le frère*
brown *marron*
brown rice *le riz complet*
browse (verb) *naviguer*
bruise *le bleu*
brunette *châtain/châtaine*
brush *la brosse*
bubblebath *le bain moussant*
bucket *le seau*
buckle *la boucle*
buffet *le buffet*
build (verb) *construire*
bulb (light) *l'ampoule (f)*
bulletin board *le panneau d'affichage*
bumper *le pare-choc*
bun *le petit gâteau*
bunch *la botte*
buoy *la bouée*
burger *le hamburger*
burgle *cambrioler*
burn *la brûlure*
bus *le bus*
bus driver *le conducteur de bus*
bus station *le dépôt*
bus stop *l'arrêt de bus (m)*
bus ticket *le ticket*
business class *la classe affaires*
business, on *pour affaires*
bust *le buste*
butcher's *la boucherie*
butter *le beurre*
button *le bouton*
buy (verb) *acheter*
by *par*

C

cabin *la cabine*
cable *le câble*
cable car *le téléphérique*
cable television *la télévision par câble*
café *le café*
cake *le gâteau*
calculator *la calculatrice*
calendar *le calendrier*
call button *le bouton d'appel*
calm *calme*
camera *l'appareil photo (m)*
camera bag *l'étui pour appareil photo (m)*
camera case *le sac pour appareil photo*
camisole *le caraco*
camp (verb) *camper*
camper van *la caravane*
camper van site *le terrain pour caravanes*
camping kettle *la bouilloire de camping*
camping stove *le réchaud*
campsite *le (terrain de) camping*
can *la boîte de conserve*
can (verb) *pouvoir*
Canada *le Canada*
candy *les bonbons (m pl)*
can opener *l'ouvre-boîte (m)*
capital *la capitale*
cappuccino *le cappuccino*
capsule *la capsule*
car *la voiture*
car accident *l'accident de voiture (m)*
car crash *l'accident de voiture (m)*
card *la carte*
cardboard *le carton*
cardigan *le cardigan; le gilet*

cards *les cartes (f pl)*
carnival *le carnaval*
carpet *le tapis*
car rental *la location de voitures*
carrot *la carotte*
carry (verb) *porter*
carry out *à emporter*
cart *le chariot*
carton *la brique*
car wash *la station de lavage*
case *l'étui (m)*
cash *le liquide*
cash (verb) *encaisser*
cash machine *le distributeur*
cash register *la caisse*
casino *le casino*
casserole dish *la marmite; la cocotte*
castle *le château*
casual *décontracté/décontractée*
cat *le chat*
catamaran *le catamaran*
catch (verb) *attraper*
cathedral *la cathédrale*
cauliflower *le chou-fleur*
caution *la prudence*
cave *la caverne*
CD *le CD*
ceiling *le plafond*
celebration *la fête*
cell phone *le téléphone portable*
central heating *le chauffage central*
center *le centre*
cereal *la céréale*
chair *la chaise*
chair lift *le télésiège*
champagne *le champagne*
change (verb) *changer*
change purse *le porte-monnaie*
changing rooms *le vestiaire*

channel (TV) *la chaîne*
charge (verb) *charger*
charger (battery) *le chargeur*
chart *le tableau*
cheap *bon marché*
check *le chèque*
check (bill) *l'addition (f)*
checkbook *le chéquier*
checker *le caissier*
check in *l'enregistrement (m)*
check in (verb) *enregistrer*
check-in desk *l'enregistrement des bagages (m)*
checking account *le compte courant*
check out (hotel) *les formalités de départ (f pl)*
checkout *la caisse*
checkup *la visite de contrôle*
cheek *la joue*
cheers! *santé!*
cheese *le fromage*
chef *le chef de cuisine*
cherry *la cerise*
cherry tomato *la tomate cerise*
chest *la poitrine*
chewing gum *le chewing-gum*
chicken *le poulet*
chickpeas *les pois chiches (m pl)*
child *l'enfant (m)*
children's menu *le menu enfants*
chili pepper *le piment*
chill *le refroidissement*
chin *le menton*
chocolate *le chocolat*
choke (verb) *étouffer*
chop *la côtelette*
chorizo *le chorizo*
church *l'église (f)*
cigar *le cigare*
cigarette *la cigarette*
cilantro *la coriandre*
cinnamon *la cannelle*

circle *le cercle*
citrus fruit *les agrumes (m pl)*
city *la ville*
clean *propre*
cleaner *l'homme (m)/la femme (f) de ménage*
client *le client/la cliente*
cliff *la falaise (f)*
clinic *la clinique*
clock *l'horloge (f)*
clock radio *le radio-réveil*
close (near) *près*
close (verb) *fermer*
closed *fermé/fermée*
closet *l'armoire (f)*
clothes *les vêtements (m pl)*
cloud *le nuage*
cloudy *nuageux*
clubbing *sortir en boîte*
coach *le car*
coast *la côte*
coaster *le dessous-de-verre*
coast guard *le garde-côte; le maître-naguer sauveteur*
coat *le manteau*
coat hanger *le porte-manteau*
cockroach *le cafard*
cocktail *le cocktail*
coconut *la noix de coco*
cod *la morue; le cabillaud*
coffee *le café*
coffee cup *la tasse à café*
coffee machine *le percolateur*
coffee table *la table basse*
coin *la pièce*
colander *la passoire*
cold (adj) *froid/froide*
cold (illness) *le rhume*
color *la couleur*
colored pencil *le crayon de couleur*
college *l'université (f)*
comb *le peigne*

come (verb) *venir*
company *la société*
compartment *le compartiment*
compass *la boussole*
comforter *la couette*
complain *porter plainte*
complaint *la plainte*
computer *l'ordinateur (m)*
concert *le concert*
concourse *le hall de gare*
conditioner
  l'après-shampooing (m)
condom *le préservatif*
confident *sûr/sûre de soi*
confused *désorienté/désorientée*
connection *la correspondance*
constipation *la constipation*
construction site *le chantier*
construction worker *le maçon*
consul *le consul*
consulate *le consulat*
consultation *la consultation*
contact lenses *les lentilles
  de contact (f pl)*
contact number *le numéro
  à contacter*
container *le récipient*
contents *le contenu*
continent *le continent*
contraception *la contraception*
cookie *le biscuit*
cookie sheet *la plaque à four*
cooking *la cuisine*
cooler *la glacière*
copy (verb) *photocopier*
coral reef *le récif de corail*
core *le trognon*
cork *le bouchon*
corkscrew *le tire-bouchon*
corn *le maïs*
corner *le coin*
correct *juste*
cotton *le coton*

cough *la toux*
cough medicine *le médicament
  pour la toux*
count (verb) *compter*
counter *le jeton*
country *le pays*
couple *le couple*
courier *le coursier*
course (study) *le cours*
courses (meals) *les plats (m pl)*
courtyard *la cour*
cousin *le cousin/la cousine*
cow *la vache*
crab *le crabe*
cramp *la crampe*
cream *la crème*
credit card *la carte de crédit*
crêpes *les crêpes (f pl)*
crib *le lit bébé*
crime *le crime*
croissant *le croissant*
cross trainer *le cross trainer*
cruise *la croisière*
crushed *écrasé/écrasée*
crust *la croûte*
cry (verb) *pleurer*
cucumber *le concombre*
cufflinks *les boutons de
  manchette (m pl)*
cup *la tasse*
curly *frisé*
currency exchange
  le bureau de change
current *le courant*
curry *le curry*
curtain *le rideau*
cushion *le coussin*
customer *le client/la cliente*
customs *la douane*
cut *la coupure*
cutlery *les couverts (m pl)*
cutting board *la planche
  à découper*

cycle (verb) *faire du vélo*
cycle lane *la piste cyclable*
cycling helmet *le casque de vélo*

D

dairy *la crémerie*
damaged *endommagé/endommagée*
dance *la danse*
dancing *danser*
danger *le danger*
dark *foncé/foncée*
dashboard *le tableau de bord*
daughter *la fille*
day *le jour*
day planner *l'agenda (m)*
debit card *la carte bancaire*
December *décembre*
deck chair *le transat*
deep-fried *frit/frite*
degrees *les degrés (m pl)*
delay *le retard*
delayed *retardé/retardée*
delicatessen *la charcuterie*
delicious *délicieux/délicieuse*
delivery *la livraison (f)*
dentist *le/la dentiste*
deodorant *le déodorant*
department store *le grand magasin*
departure board *le tableau des départs*
departure lounge *la salle d'embarquement*
departures *les départs (m pl)*
deposit *la caution*
deposit (verb) *déposer*
desert *le désert*
desk *le bureau*
dessert *le dessert*

dessertspoon *la cuillère à dessert*
destination *la destination*
detergent *le produit de nettoyage*
develop (a film) *développer*
diabetic *diabétique*
dial (verb) *composer*
diaper *la couche*
diarrhea *la diarrhée*
dictionary *le dictionnaire*
diesel *le diesel; le gazole*
difficult *difficile*
digital camera *l'appareil photo numérique (m)*
digital radio *la radio numérique*
dinghy *le bateau gonflable*
dining car *le wagon-restaurant*
dining room *la salle à manger*
dinner *le dîner*
dirty *sale*
disabled parking *la place de parking réservée aux handicapés*
disabled person *le handicapé*
discuss (verb) *discuter*
disembark (verb) *débarquer*
dish *le plat*
dishes *la vaisselle*
dishwasher *le lave-vaisselle*
distance *la distance*
dive (verb) *plonger*
divorced *divorcé/divorcée*
do (verb) *faire*
doctor *le médecin*
doctor's office *le cabinet médical*
dog *le chien*
doll *la poupée*
dolphin *le dauphin*

don't *ne…pas*
door *la porte*
doorbell *la sonnette*
dosage *la posologie*
double bed *le lit à deux places*
double room *la chambre pour deux personnes*
down *en bas*
download (verb) *télécharger*
drain *l'égout (m)*
draw (verb) *dessiner*
drawer *le tiroir*
drawing *le dessin*
dress *la robe*
drink (noun) *la boisson*
drink (verb) *boire*
drive (verb) *conduire*
driver *le conducteur*
driver's license *le permis de conduire*
drugstore *la pharmacie*
dry *sec/sèche*
duck *le canard*
duffel bag *le fourre-tout*
during *pendant*
dust pan *la pelle*
duty-free store *le magasin hors taxe*
DVD *le DVD*
DVD player *le lecteur de DVD*

E

each *chaque*
ear *l'oreille (f)*
early *tôt*
earrings *les boucles d'oreille (f pl)*
earthquake *le tremblement de terre*
east *l'est (m)*
easy *facile*
eat (verb) *manger*

eat in *manger sur place*
eat out *sortir manger*
egg *l'œuf (m)*
eggplant *l'aubergine (f)*
elbow *le coude*
electric razor *le rasoir électrique*
electrician *l'électricien (m)*
electricity *l'électricité (f)*
elevator *l'ascenseur (m)*
email *l'e-mail (m)*
email address *l'adresse e-mail (f)*
embarrassed *gêné/gênée*
embassy *l'ambassade (f)*
emergency *l'urgence (f)*
emergency exit *la sortie de secours*
emergency room *la salle des urgences*
emergency services *les services d'urgence (m pl)*
emigrate (verb) *émigrer*
empty *vide*
end *la fin*
engaged *occupé/occupée*
engine *le moteur*
English *anglais/anglaise*
engraving *la gravure*
entrance *l'entrée (f)*
entrance ramp *la bretelle d'accès*
entrance ticket *le billet d'entrée*
envelope *l'enveloppe (f)*
epileptic *épileptique*
equipment *l'équipement (m)*
espresso *l'expresso (m)*
euro *l'euro (m)*
evening *le soir*
evening dress *la robe de soirée*
evening menu *le menu du soir*
events *les épreuves (f pl)*
every *chaque*
exactly *exactement*

examine (verb) *examiner*
exchange rate *le taux de change*
excited *excité/excitée*
excuse me *pardon*
exercise bike *le vélo d'appartement*
exhaust (car) *le pot d'échappement*
exhibition *l'exposition (f)*
exit *la sortie*
expensive *cher/chère*
expiration date *la date d'expiration*
express service *le service rapide*
extension cord *la rallonge*
extra *en plus*
eye *l'œil (m)*
eyebrow *le sourcil*
eyelash *le cil*
eyeliner *l'eye-liner (m)*

F

fabric *le tissu*
face *le visage*
faint (verb) *s'évanouir*
fairground *la fête foraine*
fall *l'automne (m)*
family *la famille*
family room *la chambre familiale*
family ticket *le billet famille*
fan *le ventilateur*
far *loin*
fare *le prix*
farm *la ferme*
farmer *l'agriculteur/l'agricultrice (m/f)*
fashion *la mode*
fast *vite*
fast food *la restauration rapide*
fat *le gras*
father *le père*

faucet *le robinet*
favorite *préféré/préférée*
February *février*
feel (verb) *se sentir*
female *la femme*
fence *la clôture*
ferry *le ferry*
festivals *les fêtes (f pl)*
fever *la fièvre*
field *le champ*
fillet *le filet*
film (camera) *la pellicule*
find (verb) *trouver*
fine (legal) *l'amende (f)*
finger *le doigt*
finish (verb) *finir*
fins *les palmes (f pl)*
fire *l'incendie (m)*
fire alarm *l'alarme incendie (f)*
fire department *les pompiers (m pl)*
fire engine *le camion de pompiers*
fire escape *l'escalier de secours (m)*
fire extinguisher *l'extincteur (m)*
fire hydrant *la bouche d'incendie*
first *premier/première*
first aid *les premiers secours (m pl)*
first-aid box *la trousse de premiers secours*
fish *les poissons (m pl)*
fishing *la pêche*
fishing rod *la canne à pêche*
fish seller *le poissonnier*
fitness *la forme physique*
fitting room *cabines d'essayage; le vestiaire* **fix (verb)** *réparer*
flag *le drapeau*
flash gun *le flash*
flashlight *la lampe torche; la lampe de poche*

flat tire *la crevaison; le pneu crevé*
flight *le vol*
flight attendant *l'hôtesse de l'air (f)/le steward (m)*
flight number *le numéro de vol*
flip-flops *les tongs (f pl)*
flood *l'inondation (f)*
floor *le sol*
florist *le/la fleuriste (m/f)*
flowers *les fleurs (f pl)*
flu *la grippe*
fly (verb) *prendre l'avion*
fog *le brouillard*
food *la nourriture*
foot *le pied*
footpath *le sentier*
for *pour*
foreign currency *les devises étrangères (f pl)*
forest *la forêt*
fork *la fourchette*
form *la fiche*
fortnight *quinze jours*
forward *l'avant (m)*
fountain *la fontaine*
fracture *la fracture*
fragile *fragile*
frame *le cadre*
France *la France*
free *libre*
free (no charge) *gratuit/gratuite*
freeze (verb) *geler*
French *français/française*
French fries *frites*
French press *la cafetière*
fresh *frais/fraîche*
Friday *vendredi*
fried *frit/frite*
friend *l'ami/amie (m/f)*
from *de*
front door *la porte d'entrée*
front; in front of *devant*

frost *le givre*
frozen *surgelé/surgelée*
fruit *les fruits (m pl)*
fry (verb) *frire*
frying pan *la poêle*
fuel gauge *la jauge à essence*
full (glass) *plein/pleine*
full (hotel) *complet/complète*
furniture store *le magasin de meubles*
fuse box *le tableau électrique*

G

game *le jeu; le match*
garage *le garage*
garden *le jardin*
garlic *l'ail (m)*
gas (heating) *le gaz*
gasoline *l'essence (f)*
gas station *la station-service*
gate *le portail*
gear shift *le levier de vitesses*
get (to fetch) *aller chercher*
get (to obtain) *obtenir*
gift *le cadeau*
gift store *la boutique de souvenirs/cadeaux*
gift-wrap *emballer dans du papier-cadeau*
gin *le gin*
ginger *le gingembre*
giraffe *la girafe*
girl *la fille*
girlfriend *la copine*
give (verb) *donner*
glass *le verre*
glasses *les lunettes (f pl)*
gloss *brillant/brillante*
gloves *les gants (m pl)*
glue *la colle*
go (verb) *aller*
go out (verb) *sortir*
goggles *les lunettes (f pl)*

gold l'or (m)
golf le golf
golf ball la balle de golf
golf club le club de golf
golf course le terrain
   de golf
golf tee le té de golf
good bon/bonne
good afternoon bonjour
goodbye au revoir
good evening bonsoir
good morning bonjour
good night bonne nuit
GPS receiver le GPS
gram le gramme
grater la râpe
graze l'égratignure (f)
gray gris/grise
Great Britain
   la Grande-Bretagne
green vert/verte
green slope la piste verte
green tea le thé vert
griddle pan le gril
grocer l'épicier (m)
groceries
   les provisions (f pl)
ground moulu/moulue
group le groupe
guarantee la garantie
guest l'invité/l'invitée (m/f)
guide le/la guide
guidebook le guide
guided tour la visite guidée
gym la gym

H

hail la grêle
hair les cheveux (m pl)
hairdresser's le salon de coiffure
half la moitié
hand la main
handbag le sac à main

handle la poignée
hand luggage le bagage à main
happen (verb) se passer
happy heureux/heureuse
harbor le port
hard dur/dure
hardware store la quincaillerie
hat le chapeau
hatchback le hayon
hate (verb) détester
have (verb) avoir
hayfever le rhume des foins
hazard lights les feux
   de détresse (m pl)
he il
head la tête
headache le mal de tête
headlight le phare
headphones les écouteurs (m pl)
head rest l'appuie-tête (m)
health la santé
health insurance
   l'assurance maladie (f)
hear (verb) entendre
heart le cœur
heart condition
   le problème cardiaque
heater le chauffage
heavy lourd/lourde
heel le talon
height la hauteur
hello salut
helmet le casque
help l'assistance (f)
help (verb) aider
her elle; son/sa/ses
herb l'herbe aromatique (f)
here ici
high blood pressure
   l'hypertension (f)
high chair la chaise haute
high-speed train le TGV
highway l'autoroute (f)

hiking *faire de la randonnée*
hiking boots *les chaussures de marche (f pl)*
hill *la colline*
him *lui*
hip *la hanche*
hockey *le hockey*
hold (verb) *tenir*
home *à la maison*
hood *la capuche*
hood (car) *le capot*
horn *le klaxon*
horse *le cheval*
horseback riding *l'équitation (f)*
hospital *l'hôpital (m)*
host *l'hôte/hôtesse (m/f)*
hot *chaud/chaude*
hot (spicy) *épicé/épicée*
hot chocolate *le chocolat chaud*
hot drinks *les boissons chaudes (f pl)*
hotel *l'hôtel (m)*
hour *l'heure (f)*
house *la maison*
hovercraft *l'aéroglisseur (m)*
how? *comment?*
how many? *combien?*
humid *humide*
hundred *cent*
hurricane *l'ouragan (m)*
husband *le mari*
hydrofoil *l'hydroglisseur (m)*

I

I (1st person) *je*
ice *la glace*
ice (cube) *le glaçon*
ice (on the road) *le verglas*
ice cream *la glace*
ice-skating *le patinage*
icy *verglacé/verglacée*
ID *la pièce d'identité*
illness *la maladie*
immigration *l'immigration (f)*
in *dans*
inbox *la boîte de réception*
inch *le pouce*
indoor pool *la piscine couverte*
infection *l'infection (f)*
in-flight meal *le repas à bord*
inhaler *l'inhalateur (m)*
injection *la piqûre*
injure *blesser*
injury *la blessure*
insect repellent *l'insectifuge (m)*
inside *à l'intérieur de*
instructions *le mode d'emploi*
insurance *l'assurance (f)*
insurance company *la compagnie d'assurance*
insurance policy *la police d'assurance*
intensive care unit *l'unité de soins intensifs (f)*
interesting *intéressant/intéressante*
internet *l'internet (m)*
internet café *le cybercafé*
interpreter *l'interprète (m/f)*
into *dans*
inventory *l'inventaire (m)*
invoice *la facture*
iron *le fer à repasser*
ironing board *la planche à repasser*
island *l'île (f)*
it *il/elle*

J

jacket *la veste*
jam *la confiture*
January *janvier*
jar *le pot*
jaw *la mâchoire*
jazz club *le club
  de jazz*
jeans *le jean*
jellyfish *la méduse*
jet skiing *le jet-ski*
jeweler *la bijouterie*
jewelry *les bijoux (m pl)*
jogging *le jogging*
juice *le jus*
July *juillet*
jumper *le pull*
June *juin*

K

kayak *le kayak*
keep (verb)
  garder; rester
ketchup *le ketchup*
kettle *la bouilloire*
key *la clé*
keyboard *le clavier*
kilo *le kilo*
kilogram *le kilogramme*
kilometer *le kilomètre*
kitchen *la cuisine*
knee *le genou*
knife *le couteau*
knock down *renverser*
know (a fact) *savoir*
know (people)
  connaître

L

label *l'étiquette (f)*
lake *le lac*
lamb *l'agneau (m)*
laptop *l'ordinateur portable (m)*

large *grand/grande*
last *dernier/dernière*
last week *la semaine dernière*
late *tard; en retard*
laugh (verb) *rire*
laundromat *la laverie automatique*
lawyer *l'avocat/avocate (m/f)*
leak *la fuite*
learn (verb) *apprendre*
leave (verb) *partir*
left (direction) *la gauche; à gauche*
left luggage *la consigne*
leg *la jambe*
leisure *le temps libre*
leisure activities *les loisirs (m pl)*
lemon *le citron*
lemonade *la limonade*
lemon grass *la citronnelle*
length *la longueur*
lens *l'objectif (m)*
lettuce *la laitue*
library *la bibliothèque*
lid *le couvercle*
lifeguard *le sauveteur*
life jacket *le gilet de sauvetage*
life ring *la bouée de sauvetage*
lift pass *le forfait*
light *léger/légère*
light (noun) *la lumière*
light (verb) *allumer*
light bulb *l'ampoule (f)*
lighter *le briquet*
lighthouse *le phare*
like (verb) *aimer*
lime *le citron vert*
line *la ligne*
liquid *le liquide*
list *la liste*
listen (verb) *écouter*
liter *le litre*
little *petit/petite*
living room *le salon*
load (verb) *charger*

loan *le prêt*
lock (verb) *fermer à clé*
lockers *les casiers (m pl)*
log on (verb) *se connecter*
log out (verb) *se déconnecter*
long *long/longue*
look (verb) *regarder*
lose (verb) *perdre*
lost property *les objets*
  trouvés (m pl)
lounge chair *la chaise longue*
love (verb) *aimer/adorer*
low *bas/basse*
luggage *les bagages (m pl)*
luggage rack *le porte-bagages*
lunch *le déjeuner*
lunch menu *le menu du déjeuner*

M

machine *la machine*
magazine *le magazine*
mail (verb) *poster*
mailbox *la boîte aux lettres*
mail carrier *le facteur*
main course *le plat principal*
make (verb) *faire*
makeup *le maquillage*
mallet *le maillet*
man *l'homme (m)*
manager *le/la chef (m/f)*
mango *la mangue*
manicure *la manucure; le soin*
  des mains
manual *le manuel*
manuscript *le manuscrit*
many *beaucoup*
map *la carte; le plan*
March *mars*
marina *le port de plaisance*
market *le marché*
marmalade
  la confiture d'oranges
married *marié/mariée*

mascara *le mascara*
massage *le massage*
match (light) *l'allumette (f)*
match (sport) *le match*
matte *mat/mate*
mattress *le matelas*
May *mai*
maybe *peut-être*
mayonnaise *la mayonnaise*
meal *le repas*
measure *la mesure*
meat *la viande*
meatballs *les boulettes*
  de viande (f pl)
mechanic *le mécanicien/*
  la mécanicienne
medicine *le médicament*
medium *moyen/moyenne*
memory card *la carte mémoire*
memory stick *la clé USB*
menu *le menu*
merry-go-round *le ménage*
message *le message*
metal *le métal*
meter *le mètre*
microwave *le micro-onde*
middle *le milieu*
midnight *minuit*
migraine *la migraine*
mile *le mile*
milk *le lait*
mineral water *l'eau minérale (f)*
minibar *le minibar*
mint *la menthe*
minute *la minute*
mirror *le miroir*
mist *le brouillard*
mistake *l'erreur (f)*
mixing bowl *le bol mélangeur*
mole (medical) *le grain de beauté*
Monday *lundi*
money *l'argent (m)*
monkey *le singe*

month *le mois*
monument *le monument*
mooring *le bassin d'amarrage*
mop *la serpillère*
more *plus*
morning *le matin*
mosquito *le moustique*
mosquito net *la moustiquaire*
mother *la mère*
motorcycle *la moto*
mountain *la montagne*
mountain bike *le VTT*
mouse *la souris*
mouth *la bouche*
mouthwash *le bain de bouche*
move (verb) *bouger*
movie *le film*
movie theater *le cinéma*
mozzarella *la mozzarella*
much *beaucoup*
muffin *le muffin*
mug *le mug*
muscles *les muscles (m pl)*
museum *le musée*
mushroom *le champignon*
music *la musique*
musician *le musicien/la musicienne*
must (verb) *devoir*
mustard *la moutarde*
my *mon/ma/mes*

N

nail *l'ongle (m)*
nail scissors *les ciseaux à ongles (m pl)*
name *le nom*
napkin *la serviette*
narrow *étroit/étroite*
national park *le parc national*
natural *naturel/naturelle*
nausea *la nausée*
navigate (verb) *naviguer*

near *près de*
nearby *proche*
neck *le cou*
necklace *le collier*
need (verb) *avoir besoin de*
nervous *nerveux/nerveuse*
net *le filet*
network *le réseau*
never *jamais*
new *nouveau/nouvelle*
news *les nouvelles (f pl)*
newspaper *le journal*
newsstand *le marchand de journaux*
next *prochain/prochaine*
next week *la semaine prochaine*
nice *joli/jolie*
night *la nuit*
nightclub *la boîte de nuit*
no *non*
no entry *entrée interdite*
noisy *bruyant/bruyante*
noon *midi*
normal *normal/normale*
north *le nord*
nose *le nez*
nosebleed *le saignement de nez*
not *pas*
notebook *le carnet*
nothing *rien*
November *novembre*
now *maintenant*
number *le numéro*
number plate *la plaque d'immatriculation*
nurse *l'infirmière (f)*
nuts *fruits à coque (m pl)*

O

oar *la rame*
oats *l'avoine (f)*
occupations *les professions (f pl)*

occupied *occupé/occupée*
ocean *l'océan (m)*
October *octobre*
octopus *la pieuvre*
of *de*
office *le bureau*
often *souvent*
oil *l'huile (f)*
ointment *la pommade*
OK *d'accord*
old *vieux/vieille*
olive oil *l'huile d'olive (f)*
olives *les olives (f pl)*
omelet *l'omelette (f)*
on *sur*
one-way ticket *l'aller simple (m)*
onion *l'oignon (m)*
online *en ligne*
only *seulement*
onto *sur*
open *ouvert/ouverte*
open (verb) *ouvrir*
opening hours *les horaires d'ouverture (m pl)*
opening times *les heures d'ouverture (f pl)*
opera *l'opéra (m)*
opera house *l'opéra (m)*
operation *l'opération (f)*
opposite *en face de*
or *ou*
orange (adj) *orange*
orange (noun) *l'orange (f)*
orange juice *le jus d'orange*
order *l'ordre (m)*
order (verb) *commander*
other *autre*
our *notre/nos*
out (offside) *hors-jeu*
outdoor pool *la piscine découverte*
outside *dehors*
oven *le four*
oven mitts *les gants de cuisine (m)*

over *au-dessus de*
overdraft *le découvert*
overhead bin *le casier à bagages*
owe (verb) *devoir*

P

pack of cards *le jeu de cartes*
package *le paquet*
pajamas *le pyjama*
pail *le seau*
pain *la douleur*
painful *douleureux/douleureuse*
painkiller *l'analgésique (m)*
painting *la peinture*
pair *la paire*
pan *le plateau*
pan fried *sauté/sautée*
pants *le pantalon*
panty hose *le collant*
paper *le papier*
parents *les parents (m pl)*
park *le parc*
parka *l'anorak (m)*
parking *le stationnement*
parking lot *le parking*
parking meter *le parcmètre; l'horodateur (m)*
parmesan *le parmesan*
parsley *le persil*
partner *le/la partenaire*
pass *la passe*
pass (verb) *doubler*
passenger *le passager*
passport *le passeport*
passport control *le contrôle des passeports*
pasta *les pâtes (f pl)*
pastry *la pâte*
pastries *les pâtisseries (f pl)*
path *l'allée (f)*
patient *le patient/la patiente*
pause *la pause*

pay (verb) *payer*
payment *le paiement*
payphone *le téléphone public*
peanut *la cacahouète*
peanut butter *le beurre de cacahouètes*
pear *la poire*
pedestrian crossing *le passage piéton*
pedicure *la pédicure*
peel (verb) *éplucher*
peeler *l'éplucheur (m)*
pen *le stylo*
pencil *le crayon*
people *les gens (m pl)*
pepper *le poivre*
perfume *le parfum*
perhaps *peut-être*
pet *l'animal de compagnie (m)*
pharmacist *le pharmacien/la pharmacienne*
pharmacy *la pharmacie*
photo album *l'album photo (m)*
photo frame *le cadre*
photograph *la photo*
photography *la photographie*
pianist *le/la pianiste*
picnic *le pique-nique*
picnic basket *le panier de pique-nique*
pie *la tourte*
piece *le morceau; la part*
pill *la pilule*
pillow *l'oreiller (m)*
pilot *le/la pilote*
PIN *le code secret*
pink *rose*
pint *la pinte*
pitch *le terrain*
pitch a tent (verb) *monter une tente*
pitcher *le piche; la carafe; la cruche*

pizza *la pizza*
plane (carpentry) *le rabot*
planet *la planète*
plants *les plantes (f pl)*
plate *l'assiette (f)*
platform (rail) *le quai*
play (theater) *la pièce*
play (verb) *jouer*
playground *le terrain de jeux*
please *s'il te/vous plaît*
pleasure boat *le bateau de plaisance*
plug (electric) *la prise*
plum *la prune*
plumber *le plombier*
pocket *la poche*
point *le point*
police *la police*
police car *la voiture de police*
policeman *le policier*
police officer *l'agent de police (m/f)*
police station *le commissariat (de police)*
policewoman *la policière*
policy (insurance) *la police d'assurance*
pool (swimming) *la piscine; le bassin*
pork *le porc*
porridge *le porridge*
porter *le bagagiste*
portion *la portion*
possible *possible*
post office *la poste*
postage *le tarif d'affranchissement*
postcard *la carte postale*
potato *la pomme de terre*
potato chips *les chips (f pl)*
poultry *la volaille*
pound *la livre*
pour *verser*
powder *la poudre*

power (electric) *le courant*
power outage *la coupure de courant*
prefer (verb) *préférer*
pregnancy test *le test de grossesse*
pregnant *enceinte*
prescription (medical) *l'ordonnance (f)*
present *le cadeau*
press *la presse*
price *le prix*
price list *le tarif*
print *l'épreuve (f)*
print (photo) *la photo sur papier*
print (verb) *imprimer*
program *le programme*
proud *fier/fière*
prove (verb) *prouver*
province *la province*
public holiday *le jour férié*
pump *la pompe*
purple *violet/violette*
push *Poussez*
put (verb) *mettre*

Q

quarter *le quart*
quick *vite*

R

rabbit *le lapin*
race *la course*
racecourse *le champ de courses*
radiator *le radiateur*
radio *la radio*
rail *le rail*
railroad *le chemin de fer*
rain *la pluie*
rain boots *les bottes de caoutchouc (f pl)*
rain forest *la forêt tropicale*
rape *le viol*

rarely *rarement*
rash *l'éruption (f)*
raspberry *la framboise*
rat *le rat*
raw *cru/crue*
razor *le rasoir*
read (verb) *lire*
ready *prêt/prête*
real estate agent *l'agent immobilier (m)*
really *vraiment*
reboot (verb) *redémarrer*
receipt *le reçu*
receive (verb) *recevoir*
reception *la réception*
receptionist *le/la réceptionniste*
reclaim tag *l'étiquette (f)*
record (sports) *le record*
record store *le disquaire*
recycling bin *la boîte à déchets recyclables*
red *rouge*
reduction *la réduction*
refrigerator *le réfrigérateur; le frigo*
region *la région*
registration number *la plaque d'immatriculation*
relatives *les parents (m pl)*
release (verb) *lâcher*
remote control *la télécommande*
rent (verb) *louer*
repair (verb) *réparer*
research *la recherche*
reservation *la réservation*
reserve (verb) *réserver*
restaurant *le restaurant*
restrooms *les toilettes (f pl)*
resuscitation *la réanimation*
retired *retraité/retraitée*
return *le retour*
return ticket *l'aller-retour (m)*
reverse (verb) *faire marche arrière*

rib *la côte*
rice *le riz*
rides (fairground)
  les manèges (m pl)
right *la droite; à droite*
right (correct) *vrai/vraie*
ring *la bague*
rinse (verb) *rincer*
ripe *mûr/mûre*
river *la rivière*
road *la route*
road signs *les panneaux
  routiers (m pl)*
roads *les routes (f pl)*
roadwork *les travaux routiers
  (m pl)*
roast *le rôti*
rob *voler*
robbery *le vol*
robe *la robe*
rock climbing
  l'escalade (f)
rocks *les rochers (m pl)*
roll (of film) *la pellicule*
romantic comedy
  la comédie romantique
roof *le toit*
roofrack *la galerie*
room (hotel) *la chambre*
room (in house) *la pièce*
room key *la clef de la chambre*
room service *le service
  en chambre*
root *la racine*
rope *la corde*
round *rond/ronde*
router *le routeur*
row *la rangée*
rowing machine *le rameur*
ruby *le rubis*
rug *le tapis*
run (verb) *courir*
rush (verb) *se précipiter*

S

sad *triste*
safari park *le parc safari*
safe *en sécurité*
sailing *faire de la voile*
salad *la salade*
salami *le salami*
sales assistant *le vendeur/la
  vendeuse*
salmon *le saumon*
salt *le sel*
salted *salé/salée*
same *même*
sand *le sable*
sandal *la sandale*
sandwich *le sandwich*
sanitary napkin
  la serviette hygiénique
satellite navigation *la navigation
  par satellite*
satellite TV *la télé satellite*
Saturday *samedi*
sauce *la sauce*
saucepan *la casserole*
saucer *la soucoupe*
sauna *le sauna*
sausage *la saucisse*
sauté (verb) *faire sauter*
save (verb) *sauver*
savings account
  le compte épargne
savory *salé/salée*
say (verb) *dire*
scale *la balance*
scan *le scanner*
scared *effrayé/effrayée*
scarf *le foulard*
school *l'école (f)*
scissors *les ciseaux (m pl)*
scoop (of ice cream) *la boule*
scooter *le scooter*
score (music) *la partition*
score (sport) *le score*

scuba diving *la plongée*
sea *la mer*
seafood *les fruits de mer (m pl)*
search (verb) *chercher*
season *la saison*
seat *le siège*
second (position) *deuxième*
second (time) *la seconde*
second floor *le premier étage*
security *la sécurité*
sedan *la berline*
see (verb) *voir*
seedless *sans pépins*
seeds *les graines (f pl)*
sell *vendre*
sell-by date *la date
de péremption*
send (verb) *envoyer*
send-off *l'expulsion (f)*
senior citizen *la personne âgée*
sensitive *sensible*
sentence (law)
la condamnation
separately *séparément*
September *septembre*
serious *grave*
serve *le service*
server *le serveur/la serveuse*
services *les services (m pl)*
set *le décor*
sew (verb) *coudre*
shampoo *le shampooing*
shark *le requin*
shaving foam *la mousse
à raser*
she *elle*
sheet *le drap*
shelf *l'étagère (f)*
sherbet *le sorbet*
ship *le bateau*
shirt *la chemise*
shock *le choc*
shoe *la chaussure*

shoe store *le magasin
de chaussures*
store *le magasin*
shopping *faire les courses*
shopping center
le centre commercial
short *court/courte*
shorts *le short*
shoulder *l'épaule (f)*
shout (verb) *crier*
shower *la douche*
shower gel *le gel douche*
shy *timide*
sick *malade*
side *le côté*
side-by-side refrigerator
le réfrigérateur-congélateur
side dish *le plat
d'accompagnement*
side effect *l'effet secondaire (m)*
side order
l'accompagnement (m)
side plate *la petite assiette*
sidewalk *le trottoir*
sightseeing *le tourisme*
sign (verb) *signer*
signal *le signal*
signature *la signature*
signpost *le panneau*
silk *la soie*
silver *l'argent (m)*
singer *le chanteur/la chanteuse*
single bed *le lit simple*
single room
la chambre individuelle
sink *le lavabo; l'évier (m)*
siren *la sirène*
sister *la sœur*
size (clothes) *la taille;* **(shoes)**
la pointure
skate *le patin à glace*
sketch *le croquis*
ski *le ski*

ski (verb) *skier*
ski boot *la chaussure de ski*
ski slope *la piste de ski*
skin *la peau*
skirt *la jupe*
skis *les skis (m pl)*
sleep (verb) *dormir*
sleeper berth *la couchette*
sleeping bag
  le sac de couchage
sleeping pill *le somnifère*
slice *la part*
slickers *les imperméables
  (m pl)*
slide *le toboggan*
slip (undergarment)
  la combinaison
slippers *les pantoufles (f pl)*
slope *la pente*
slow *lent/lente*
slow down *ralentir*
small *petit/petite*
smartphone *le smartphone*
smile *le sourire*
smoke *la fumée*
smoke (verb) *fumer*
smoke alarm *le détecteur
  de fumée*
smoking area *la zone fumeur*
snack *l'en-cas (m)*
snack bar *le snack-bar*
snake *le serpent*
sneakers *les tennis (f pl);
  les baskets (f pl)*
sneeze *l'éternuement (m)*
sneeze (verb) *éternuer*
snore (verb) *ronfler*
snorkel *le tuba*
snow *la neige*
snow (verb) *neiger*
snowboard *le snowboard*
snowboarding *le surf (des neiges);
  le snowboard*

so *donc; si*
soak (verb) *laisser tremper*
soap *le savon*
soccer *le foot; le football*
socks *les chaussettes (f pl)*
soda water *le soda*
sofa *le canapé*
sofa bed *le canapé-lit*
soft *mou/molle*
soft drinks *les boissons
  non alcoolisées (f pl)*
soil *la terre*
some *quelques*
somebody *quelqu'un*
something *quelque chose*
sometimes *quelquefois*
son *le fils*
song *la chanson*
soon *bientôt*
sore *douleureux/douleureuse*
sorry *pardon; désolé/désolée*
soup *la soupe*
sour *aigre*
south *le sud*
souvenir *le souvenir*
spare tire *la roue de secours*
sparkling water *l'eau gazeuse (f)*
spatula *la spatule*
speak (verb) *parler*
speaker *le conférencier/la
  conférencière*
speciality *la spécialité*
specials *les spécialités (f pl)*
speed limit *la limitation
  de vitesse*
speedometer *le compteur
  de vitesse*
spices *les épices (f pl)*
spider *l'araignée (f)*
spinach *les épinards (m pl)*
spine *la colonne vertébrale*
splint *l'attelle (f)*
splinter *l'écharde (f)*

spoke *le rayon*

sponge *l'éponge (f)*

spoon *la cuillère*

sport *le sport*

sports center *le complexe sportif*

sprain *la foulure*

spray *le vaporisateur*

spring *le printemps*

square *le carré*

square (in town) *la place*

squash (game) *le squash*

squid *le calamar*

staff *le personnel*

stage *la scène*

staircase *l'escalier (m)*

stairs *les escaliers (m pl)*

stamp *le timbre*

start (verb) *commencer*

statement (law) *la déposition*

statue *la statue*

stay (verb) *rester*

steak *le steak; le bifteck*

steamed *cuit/cuite à la vapeur*

steering wheel *le volant*

step machine *le stepper*

stew *le ragoût*

still *encore*

sting (of insect, nettle, etc.) *la piqûre*

stir (verb) *remuer*

stir-fry *le sauté*

stolen *volé/volée*

stomach *l'estomac (m)*

stomach ache *le mal au ventre*

stone *la pierre*

stop (bus) *l'arrêt (m)*

stop (verb) *s'arrêter*

storm *la tempête*

straight *droit/droite*

straight on *tout droit*

strap *la bretelle*

strawberry *la fraise*

street *la rue*

street map *le plan*

street sign *le panneau de signalisation*

stress *le stress*

string *la ficelle*

strong *fort/forte*

student *l'étudiant/l'étudiante (m/f)*

student card *la carte d'étudiant*

study *le bureau*

stuffed animal *la peluche*

suburb *la banlieue*

subway *le métro*

subway map *le plan de métro*

suit *le costume*

suitcase *la valise*

summer *l'été (m)*

sun *le soleil*

sunbathe *prendre un bain de soleil*

sunbed *le lit de bronzage*

sunblock *l'écran total (m)*

sunburn *le coup de soleil*

Sunday *dimanche*

sunflower oil *l'huile de tournesol (f)*

sunglasses *les lunettes de soleil (f pl)*

sunhat *le chapeau (de soleil)*

sunny *ensoleillé/ensoleillée*

sunrise *le lever du soleil*

sunscreen *l'écran total (m)*

sunset *le coucher du soleil*

sunshine *le soleil*

suntan lotion *la crème solaire*

supermarket *le supermarché*

suppositories *les suppositoires (m pl)*

surf *l'écume (f)*

surf (verb) *surfer*

surfboard *la planche de surf*

surgeon *le chirurgien/ la chirurgienne*
surgery (doctor's) *le cabinet (médical)*
surgery (operation) *la chirurgie*
surprised *surpris/suprise*
sweatshirt *le sweat-shirt*
sweep (verb) *balayer*
sweet *sucré/sucrée*
sweet potato *la patate douce*
swim (verb) *nager*
swim(ming) *le baignade*
swimming cap *le bonnet de natation*
swimming pool *la piscine*
swimsuit *le maillot de bain*
swing *la balançoire*
switch (electric) *l'interrupteur (m)*

T

table *la table*
tablespoon *la cuillère à soupe*
tablet (medicine) *le cachet*
tailor *le tailleur*
take (verb) *prendre*
take off (plane) *décoller*
tall *grand/grande*
tampon *le tampon*
tan *le bronzage*
tank *le réservoir*
tax *l'impôt (m)*
taxi *le taxi*
taxi driver *le chauffeur de taxi*
taxi stand *la station de taxis*
tea *le thé*
teabag *le sachet de thé*
team *l'équipe (f)*
teapot *la théière*
teaspoon *la cuillère à café*
teeth *les dents (f pl)*
telephone *le téléphone*
telephone (verb) *téléphoner*

telephone box *la cabine téléphonique*
television *la télévision*
temperature *la température*
tennis *le tennis*
tennis ball *la balle de tennis*
tennis court *le court de tennis*
tennis racket *la raquette de tennis*
tent *la tente*
tent peg *le piquet*
terminal *le terminal*
test *l'analyse (f)*
text (SMS) *le SMS*
than *que*
thank (verb) *remercier*
thank you *merci*
that *que; ce*
the *le/la/les*
theater *le théâtre*
their *leur/leurs*
then *alors*
there *là*
there is/are *il y a*
thermometer *le thermomètre*
thermostat *le thermostat*
they *ils/elles*
thick *épais/épaisse*
thief *le voleur/la voleuse*
thin *mince*
think (verb) *penser*
this *ceci/cela/ce*
throat *la gorge*
throat lozenge *la pastille pour la gorge*
through *à travers; par*
throw *lancer*
thumb *le pouce*
Thursday *jeudi*
ticket *le billet; le ticket*
ticket gates *le portillon*
ticket inspector *le contrôleur/la contrôleuse*
ticket office *le guichet*

tie *la cravate*
tight *serré/serrée*
tile *la pièce*
time *l'heure (f)*
timetable *les horaires (m pl)*
tire *le pneu*
tire pressure *la pression des pneus*
tip *la pointe*
tissue *le kleenex*
to *à*
toast *le pain grillé*
toaster *le grille-pain*
tobacco *le tabac*
tobacconist *le bureau de tabac*
today *aujourd'hui*
toe *le doigt de pied; l'orteil (m)*
toilet paper *le rouleau de papier hygiénique*
toiletries *les accessoires de toilette (m pl)*
toll *le péage*
tomato *la tomate*
tomato sauce *le ketchup*
tomorrow *demain*
tongue *la langue*
tonight *ce soir*
too *aussi*
tooth *la dent*
toothache *le mal de dents*
toothbrush *la brosse à dents*
toothpaste *le dentifrice*
tour bus *le bus touristique*
tour guide *le guide*
tourist *le/la touriste*
tourist attraction *l'attraction touristique (f)*
tourist information *les informations touristiques (f pl)*
tourist information office *l'office du tourisme (m)*
tow *remorquer*

towards *vers*
towel *la serviette*
town *la ville*
town center *le centre-ville*
town hall *la mairie*
toy *le jouet*
track (rail) *la voie ferrée*
traffic *la circulation*
traffic circle *le rond-point*
traffic jam *le bouchon*
traffic lights *les feux (m pl)*
traffic police officer *l'agent de la circulation*
train *le train*
train station *la gare*
tram *le tram (way)*
transportation *le transport*
trash can *la poubelle*
travel (verb) *voyager*
travel agent *l'agent de voyages (m)*
travel-sickness pills *les cachets antinaupathiques (m pl)*
tray *le plateau*
tree *l'arbre (m)*
trekking *la randonnée*
trip *l'excursion (f)*
tripod *le trépied*
trout *la truite*
trunk (car) *le coffre*
try *l'essai (m)*
try (verb) *essayer*
T-shirt *le t-shirt*
tub *le pot*
tube *le tube*
Tuesday *mardi*
tumble dryer *le sèche-linge*
tuna *le thon*
turn (verb) *tourner*
tweezers *la pince à épiler*
twin beds *les lits jumeaux (m pl)*
twin room *la chambre à deux lits*

U

ugly *laid/laide*
umbrella *le parapluie*
uncle *l'oncle (m)*
under *sous*
underpass *le passage souterrain*
undershirt *le tricot de corps*
understand (verb) *comprendre*
underwear
  les sous-vêtements (m pl)
uniform *l'uniforme (m)*
United States *les États-Unis (m pl)*
unleaded *sans plomb*
until *jusqu'à*
up *en haut*
upset *contrarié/contrariée*
urgent *urgent/urgente*
us *nous*
use (verb) *utiliser*
useful *utile*
usual *habituel/habituelle*
usually *d'habitude*

V

vacancy *la place*
vacate (verb) *vider*
vacation *les vacances (f pl)*
vacuum flask
  la bouteille thermos
validate (verb) *valider*
valuables *les objets*
  de valeur (m pl)
value *la valeur*
vegetables *les légumes (m pl)*
vegetarian
  végétarien/végétarienne
veggie burger
  le hamburger végétarien
Venetian blind *le store*
very *très*
veterinarian *le/la vétérinaire*
video game *le jeu vidéo*
view *la vue*

village *le village*
vinegar *le vinaigre*
vineyard *le vignoble*
virus *le virus*
visa *le visa*
vision *la vue*
visit (verb) *visiter*
visiting hours *les horaires*
  de visite (m pl)
visitor *le visiteur*
vitamins *les vitamines (f pl)*
voice message
  le message vocal
volume *le volume*
vomit (verb) *vomir*

W

wait (verb) *attendre*
waiter *le serveur*
waiting room *la salle*
  d'attente
waitress *la serveuse*
wake up (verb) *se réveiller*
wake-up call *le réveil*
  par téléphone
walk *la promenade*
walk (verb) *marcher*
wall *le mur*
wallet *le portefeuille*
want (verb) *vouloir*
ward *le service*
warm *chaud/chaude*
wash (verb) *laver*
washing machine *le lave-linge*
wasp *la guêpe*
watch *la montre*
water *l'eau (f)*
water bottle *la bouteille d'eau*
waterfall *la cascade*
watermelon *la pastèque*
water-skiing *le ski nautique*
watersports *les sports*
  aquatiques (m pl)

water valve *l'arrivée d'eau (f)*
water wings *les brassards*
wave *la vague*
wax *l'épilation (f)*
we *nous*
weak *faible*
weather *le temps*
website *le site web*
wedding *le mariage*
Wednesday *mercredi*
week *la semaine*
weekend *le week-end*
weigh (verb) *peser*
weight *le poids*
weight allowance *le poids maximum autorisé*
welcome *bienvenue*
well *bien*
west *l'ouest (m)*
wet *mouillé/mouillée*
wetsuit *la combinaison de plongée*
wet wipe *la lingette*
whale *la baleine*
what? *quoi?*
wheat *le blé*
wheel *la roue*
wheelchair *le fauteuil roulant*
wheelchair access *l'accès handicapés (m)*
wheelchair ramp *la rampe d'accès handicapés*
when? *quand?*
where? *où?*
which? *lequel/laquelle?*
whisk *le fouet*
whiskey *le whisky*
white *blanc/blanche*
who? *qui?*
whole *entier/entière*
whole-wheat bread *le pain bis/ complet*
why? *pourquoi?*

Wi-Fi *le wifi*
wide *large*
widescreen TV *le téléviseur à écran large*
width *la largeur*
wife *la femme (f)*
win (verb) *gagner*
wind *le vent*
window *la fenêtre*
windshield *le pare-brise*
windshield wipers *les essuie-glaces (m pl)*
windsurf board *la planche à voile*
windy *il y a du vent*
wine *le vin*
wine glass *le verre à vin*
wine list *la carte des vins*
winter *l'hiver (m)*
winter sports *les sports d'hiver (m pl)*
wipe (verb) *essuyer*
with *avec*
withdraw (verb) *retirer*
withdrawal *le retrait*
without *sans*
witness (noun) *le témoin*
woman *la femme*
wood *le bois*
wool *la laine*
work *le travail*
work (verb) *travailler*
worried *inquiet/inquiète*
worse *pire*
wrapping paper *le papier-cadeau*
wrist *le poignet*
wrist watch *la montre*
write (verb) *écrire*
wrong *faux/fausse*

X

X-ray *la radio*

Y

yacht *le yacht*
year *l'année (f)*
yellow *jaune*
yes *oui*
yesterday *hier*
yoga *le yoga*
yogurt *le yaourt*
you *tu/vous*

young *jeune*
your *ton/ta/tes/ votre/vos*

Z

zero *zéro*
zipper *la fermeture éclair*
zone *la zone*
zoo *le zoo*
zucchini *la courgette*

DICTIONARY FRENCH–ENGLISH

The gender of French nouns is shown by the abbreviations (m) for masculine nouns and (f) for feminine nouns. Where nouns are in the plural; the gender is indicated by the abbreviations (m pl) or (f pl). French adjectives change according to gender and number. Here the singular masculine form is shown first; followed by the singular feminine form.

A

à *at; to*
abeille (f) *bee*
à bord *on board*
abricot (m) *apricot*
accès handicapés (m)
   wheelchair access
accessoires de toilette (m pl)
   toiletries
accident (m) *accident*
accident de voiture (m)
   car crash
accompagnement (m)
   side order
accouchement (m) *childbirth*
accoudoir (m) *arm rest*
accusation (f) *charge*
acheter *to buy*
à côté *beside*
acte de naissance (m)
   birth certificate
acteur (m) *actor*
activités (f pl) *activities*
actrice (f) *actress*
addition (f) *bill; check*
additionner *to add*
adorer *to love*
adresse (f) *address*
adresse e-mail (f)
   email address
à droite *right*
adulte (m/f) *adult*

à emporter *carry out*
aérobic (f) *aerobics*
aéroglisseur (m) *hovercraft*
aéroport (m) *airport*
affaires (f pl) *business;*
   pour affaires *on business*
à gauche *left*
agenda (m) *day planner*
agent de la circulation
   traffic police officer
agent de voyages (m)
   travel agent
agent immobilier (m)
   real estate agent
agneau (m) *lamb*
agriculteur/agricultrice (m/f)
   farmer
agrumes (m pl) *citrus*
   fruit
aide (f) *help*
aider *to help*
aigre *sour*
ail (m) *garlic*
aimer *to like; to love*
airbag (m) *airbag*
aire (f) *area*
alarme incendie (f)
   fire alarm
album photo (m)
   photo album
à l'intérieur de *inside*
allée (f) *aisle*

aller *to go*
aller simple (m)
  one-way ticket
aller-retour (m)
  return ticket
allergie (f) *allergy*
allergique *allergic*
allumer *to light*
allumette (f) *match*
alors *then*
altitude (f) *altitude*
amande (f) *almond*
ambassade (f) *embassy*
ambulance (f) *ambulance*
amende (f) *fine (legal)*
amer/amère *bitter*
ami (m)/amie (f) *friend*
ampoule (f) *blister*
ampoule (f) *light bulb*
amuse-gueule (m pl)
  bar snacks
amuser: s'amuser *to have
  a good time*
analgésique (m) *painkiller*
analyse (f) *test*
analyse sanguine (f)
  blood test
anglais/anglaise *English*
animal (m) *animal*
animal de compagnie (m)
  pet
animaux (m pl) *animals*
année (f) *year*
anniversaire (m) *birthday*
anorak (m) *parka*
antibiotique (m) *antibiotic*
antiseptique (m) *antiseptic*
août *August*
appareil photo (m) *camera*
appareil photo numérique (m)
  digital camera
apparence (f) *appearance*
appartement (m) *flat; apartment*

applaudir *to applaud*
application (f) *application*
apprendre *to learn*
appui-tête (m) *head rest*
après *after*
après-midi (m) *afternoon*
après-shampooing (m)
  conditioner
après-soleil (m) *aftersun*
araignée (f) *spider*
arbre (m) *tree*
arc (m) *arc*
arche (f) *arch*
architecte (m/f) *architect*
architecture (f) *architecture*
argent (m) *money*
armoire (f) *closet*
arrivée (f) *arrival*
arrivée d'eau (f) *water valve*
arrivées (f pl) *arrivals hall*
arriver *to arrive*
arrêt (m) *stop*
arrêt de bus (m) *bus stop*
arrêter: s'arrêter *to stop*
art (m) *art*
arthrite (f) *arthritis*
artiste peintre (m/f) *artist*
ascenceur (m) *elevator*
asseoir: s'asseoir *to sit*
assiette (f) *plate*
assistance (f) *help*
assistant/assistante (m/f)
  assistant
assister à *to attend*
assurance (f) *insurance*
assurance maladie (f)
  health insurance
asthme (m) *asthma*
athlète (m/f) *athlete*
à travers *across*
attaque (f) *attack*
attelle (f) *splint*
attendre *to wait*

attraction touristique (f)
tourist attraction
attractions (f pl)
attractions
attraper *to catch*
au revoir *goodbye*
au-delà de *beyond*
au-dessus de *above*
aubergine (f) *eggplant*
aujourd'hui *today*
aussi *too*
Australie (f) *Australia*
automatique *automatic*
automne (m) *fall*
autoroute (f) *highway*
autour de *around*
autre *other*
avant *before*
avec *with*
avenue (f) *avenue*
avion (m) *airplane*
avocat (m) *avocado*
avocat/avocate (m/f) *lawyer*
avoine (f) *oats*
avoir *to have;*
  avoir besoin de *to need*
avril *April*

B

badminton (m) *badminton*
bagage à main (m)
  hand luggage
bagages (m pl) *luggage*
bague (f) *ring*
baguette (f) *baguette*
baie (f) *berry*
baignade (f) *swimming; bathing*
baignoire (f) *bathtub*
bain (m) *bath*
bain de bouche (m) *mouthwash*
bain moussant (m)
  bubblebath
balai (m) *broom*

balai d'essuie-glace (m)
  windscreen wiper blade
balance (f) *scale*
balançoire (f) *swing*
balayer *to sweep*
balcon (m) *balcony;*
  gallery (theater)
baleine (f) *whale*
balle de golf (f) *golf ball*
balle de tennis (f) *tennis
  ball*
ballet (m) *ballet*
ballon de plage (m)
  beach ball
banane (f) *banana*
banc (m) *bench*
bandage (m) *bandage*
banlieue (f) *suburb*
banque (f) *bank*
banquier (m) *bank manager*
bar (m) *bar*
barbecue (m) *barbecue*
barman (m) *bartender*
barque (f) *rowing boat*
bas/basse *low*
basilic (m) *basil*
baskets (m pl) *sneakers*
bassin (m) *pool*
bassin d'amarrage (m)
  mooring
bateau (m) *boat*
bateau à voile
  sailing boat
bateau de plaisance (m)
  pleasure boat
bateau gonflable (m)
  dinghy
bâtons (de ski) (m pl) *ski poles*
batterie (électrique) (f)
  battery
beau/belle *beautiful*
beaucoup de *many; much*
bébé (m) *baby*

berline (f) *sedan*
besoin (m) *need*
betterave (f) *beet*
beurre (m) *butter*
beurre de cacahouètes (m)
  peanut butter
bibliothèque (f) *library*
bidet (m) *bidet*
bien *good; well*
bientôt *soon*
bienvenue *welcome*
bière (f) *beer*
bijouterie (f) *jewelry store*
bijoux (m pl) *jewelry*
bikini (m) *bikini*
billet (m) *ticket*
billet d'entrée (m)
  entrance ticket
billet familial (m) *family ticket*
biscuit (m) *cookie*
blanc/blanche *white*
blé (m) *wheat*
blesser *to injure*
blessure (f) *injury*
bleu/bleue *blue*
blocage (m) *block*
blond/e *blonde*
bœuf (m) *beef*
boire *to drink*
bois (m) *wood*
boisson (f) *drink (noun)*
boissons alcoolisées (f pl)
  alcoholic drinks
boissons chaudes (f pl)
  hot drinks
boissons non alcoolisées (f pl)
  soft drinks
boîte (f) *box*
boîte à déchets recyclables (f)
  recycling bin
boîte à fusibles (f) *fuse box*
boîte aux lettres (f)
  mailbox

boîte de conserve (f)
  can; tin
boîte de nuit (f) *nightclub*
boîte de réception (f) *inbox*
bol (m) *bowl*
bol mélangeur (m)
  mixing bowl
bon/bonne *good*
bon marché *cheap*
bonbons (m pl) *candy*
Bonjour *good morning*
Bonne nuit *goodnight*
bonnet de natation (m)
  swimming cap
bonsoir *good evening*
botte (f) *boot (footwear)*
botte (f) *bunch (herbs; vegetables)*
bottes de caoutchouc (f pl) *rain*
  boots
bouche (f) *mouth;*
bouche d'incendie (f) *fire hydrant*
boucherie (f) *butcher's*
bouchon (m) *cork*
bouchon (m) *traffic jam*
boucle (f) *buckle*
boucle d'oreille (f) *earring*
bouée (f) *bouy*
bouée de sauvetage (f)
  life ring
bouillir *to boil*
bouilloire (f) *kettle*
boulangerie (f) *bakery*
boule de glace (f)
  scoop of ice cream
boulettes de viande (f pl)
  meatballs
boussole (f) *compass*
bouteille d'eau (f)
  water bottle
bouteille Thermos (f)
  vacuum flask
bouton (m) *button*
bouton d'appel (m) *call button*

boutons de manchette (m pl)
cufflinks
bouteille (f) *bottle*
boutique (f) *boutique*
bowling (m) *bowling*
bracelet (m) *bracelet*
branche (f) *branch*
bras (m) *arm*
bretelle (f) *strap*
bretelle d'accès (f)
entrance ramp
brillant/brillante *gloss*
brioche (f) *brioche*
brique (f) *brick*
brique (f) *carton*
briquet (m) *lighter*
britannique *British*
brocoli (m) *broccoli*
bronzage (m) *tan*
brosse (f) *brush*
brosse à dents (f)
toothbrush
brosser *to brush*
brouillard (m) *mist*
brûlure (f) *burn*
bruyant/bruyante *noisy*
buffet (m) *buffet*
buffet du petit déjeuner (m)
breakfast buffet
bureau (m) *desk*
bureau (m) *office*
bureau de change (m)
currency exchange
bureau de tabac (m)
tobacconist's
bus (m) *bus*
buste (m) *bust; chest*

C

cabillaud (m) *cod*
cabine (f) *cabin*
cabine téléphonique (f)
telephone box

cabines d'essayage (pl)
fitting rooms
cabinet (m) *office*
cabinet médical (m)
doctor's office
câble (m) *cable*
cacahouète (f) *peanut*
cachet (médical) (m) *tablet*
cachets antinaupathiques
(m pl) *travel-sickness pills*
cadeau (m) *gift; present*
cadre (m) *photo frame*
cafard (m) *cockroach*
cafetière (f) *French press*
café (m) *café*
café (m) *coffee*
caisse (f) *cash register; checkout*
caissier (m) *checker*
calculatrice (f) *calculator*
calendrier (m) *calendar*
calme *calm*
cambrioler *to burgle*
camion (m) *lorry; truck*
camion de pompiers (m)
fire engine
camper *to camp*
Canada (m) *Canada*
canapé (m) *sofa*
canapé-lit (m) *sofa bed*
canard (m) *duck*
canne à pêche (f) *fishing rod*
cannelle (f) *cinnamon*
canoë (m) *canoe*
capitale (f) *capital*
capsule (f) *capsule*
capuche (f) *hood*
car (m) *coach*
caraco (m) *camisole*
carafe (f) *pitcher*
caravane (f) *camper van*
cardigan (m) *cardigan*
carnaval (m) *carnival*
carnet (m) *notebook*

carotte (f) *carrot*
carré (m) *square*
carte (f) *card*
carte (f) *map*
carte bancaire (f) *debit card*
carte de crédit (f) *credit card*
carte d'embarquement (f) *boarding pass*
carte d'étudiant (f) *student card*
carte de téléphone (f) *phone card*
carte mémoire (f) *memory card*
carte postale (f) *postcard*
carte des vins (f) *wine list*
carton (m) *cardboard*
cascade (f) *waterfall*
casier à bagages (m) *overhead bin*
casiers (m pl) *lockers*
casino (m) *casino*
casque de vélo (m) *cycling helmet*
cassé/cassée *broken*
casserole (f) *saucepan*
cassis (m) *blackcurrant*
catamaran (m) *catamaran*
cathédrale (f) *cathedral*
caution (f) *deposit*
caverne (f) *cave*
CD (m) *CD*
ce *this*
ceci *this*
ceinture (f) *belt*
cela *that*
cendrier (m) *ashtray*
cent *hundred*
centre (m) *center*
centre commercial (m) *shopping mall*

centre-ville (m) *town center*
cercle (m) *circle*
céréale (f) *cereal*
cerise (f) *cherry*
cerveau (m) *brain*
chaîne (de télé) (f) *(TV) channel*
chaise (f) *chair*
chaise haute (f) *high chair*
chaise longue (f) *lounge chair*
chaise roulante (f) *wheelchair*
chambre (f) *room; bedroom*
chambre à deux lits (f) *twin room*
chambre avec le petit déjeuner (f) *bed and breakfast*
chambre d'hôtes (f) *guesthouse; B & B*
chambre familiale (f) *family room*
chambre pour deux personnes (f) *double room*
champ (m) *field*
champagne (m) *champagne*
champ de courses (m) *racecourse*
champignon (m) *mushroom*
changer *to change*
se changer *change clothes*
chanson (f) *song*
chanteur/chanteuse (m/f) *singer*
chantier (m) *construction site*
chapeau (m) *hat*
chapeau de soleil (m) *sun hat*
chaque *each*
charger *to load; to charge (battery)*
chargeur (m) *(battery) charger*
chariot (m) *trolley*
chat (m) *cat*
châtain/châtaine *brown*

château (m) *castle*
chaud/chaude *hot*
chauffeur de taxi (m)
  taxi driver
chaussette (f) *sock*
chaussure (f) *shoe*
chaussures de marche (f pl)
  hiking boots
chef (m) *manager*
chef de cuisine (m) *chef*
chemin (m) *way*
chemin de fer (m)
  railroad
chemise (f) *shirt*
chemisier (m) *blouse*
cher/chère *expensive*
chercher *to search*
chèque (m) *check*
chéquier (m) *book*
cheval (m) *horse*
cheveux (m pl) *hair*
chien (m) *dog*
chips (f pl) *potato chips*
chirurgie (f) *surgery (operation)*
chirurgien (m) *surgeon*
choc (m) *shock*
chocolat (m) *chocolate*
chocolat chaud (m)
  hot chocolate
chou-fleur (m)
  cauliflower
cigare (m) *cigar*
cigarette (f) *cigarette*
cil (m) *eyelash*
cinq *five*
cinéma (m) *movie theater*
circulation (f) *traffic*
ciseaux (m pl) *scissors*
ciseaux à ongles (m pl)
  nail scissors
citron (m) *lemon*
citronnelle (f) *citronella;*
  lemon grass

classe affaires (f)
  business class
clavier (m) *keyboard*
clé USB (f) *memory stick*
client (m) *customer*
client (m) *guest*
climatisation (f)
  air-conditioning
clinique (f) *clinic*
clôture (f) *fence*
club de golf (m) *golf club*
club de jazz (m) *jazz club*
cocktail (m) *cocktail*
cocotte (f) *casserole dish*
code secret (m) *PIN number*
cœur (m) *heart*
coffre (m) *trunk (car);*
  safe (bank)
coiffeur/coiffeuse (m/f)
  hairdresser
coin (m) *corner*
collant (m) *panty hose*
colle (f) *glue*
collier (m) *necklace*
colline (f) *hill*
colonne vertébrale (f) *spine*
combinaison de plongée (f)
  wetsuit
commander *to order*
comme *as; like*
commencer *to start*
comment? *how?*
commissariat de police (m)
  police station
compagnie d'assurances (f)
  insurance company
compartiment (m)
  compartment
complet/complète *full (hotel)*
complexe sportif (m)
  sports center
composer *to dial*
comprendre *to understand*

compte courant (m)
  checking account
compte d'épargne (m)
  savings account
compte en banque (m)
  bank account
compter *to count*
compteur de vitesse (m)
  speedometer
comédie romantique (f)
  romantic comedy
concert (m) *concert*
concombre (m) *cucumber*
conducteur (m) *driver*
conducteur de bus (m)
  bus driver
conduire *to drive*
conférencier/conférencière (m/f)
  speaker
confiant/confiante *confident*
confiture (f) *jam*
connaître *to know*
connecter: se connecter
  (informatique) *to log on*
consigne (f) *left luggage*
constipation (f) *constipation*
construire *to build*
consul (m) *consul*
consulat (m) *consulate*
consultation (f) *consultation*
contenu (m) *contents*
continent (m) *continent*
contraception (f)
  contraception
contrarié/contrariée *upset*
contrôle des passeports (m)
  passport control
contrôleur (m)
  ticket inspector
copain (m) *friend*
copine (f) *friend*
corde (f) *rope*
coriandre (f) *cilantro*

corps (m) *body*
correspondance (f)
  connection (train)
costume (m) *suit*
côte (f) *coast*
côte (f) *rib*
côté (m) *side*
côtelette (f) *chop*
coton (m) *cotton*
cou (m) *neck*
couche (f) *diaper*
coucher de soleil (m) *sunset*
couchette (f) *sleeper berth*
coude (m) *elbow*
coudre *to sew*
couette (f) *comforter*
couleur (f) *color*
coup de fil (m) *phone call*
coup de soleil (m) *sunburn*
coupe-ongle (m) *nail clipper*
couple (m) *couple*
coupure (f) *cut*
coupure de courant (f)
  power outage
cour (f) *courtyard*
courant (électrique) (m) *power*
courgette (f) *zucchini*
cours (m) *course*
course (f) *race*
court/courte *short*
court de tennis (m)
  tennis court
cousin (m) *cousin*
coussin (m) *cushion*
couteau (m) *knife*
couvercle (m) *lid*
couverture (f) *blanket*
crabe (m) *crab*
crampe (f) *cramp*
cravate (f) *tie*
crayon (m) *pencil*
crayon de couleur (m)
  colored pencil

crème (f) *cream*
crème solaire (f) *suntan lotion*
crémerie (f) *dairy*
crêpes (f pl) *crêpes*
crevaison (f) *flat tire*
crier *to shout*
crime (m) *crime*
croisière (f) *cruise*
croissant (m) *croissant*
croquis (m) *sketch*
croûte (f) *crust*
cru/crue *raw*
cruche (f) *jug*
cuillère (f) *spoon*
cuillère à café (f) *teaspoon*
cuillère à dessert (f) *dessert spoon*
cuillère à soupe (f) *tablespoon*
cuire au four *to bake*
cuisine (f) *cooking*
cuisine (f) *kitchen*
cuit à la vapeur *steamed*
cybercafé (m) *internet café*

D

D'accord *OK*
danger (m) *danger*
dans *in; into*
danse (f) *dance*
danser *to dance*
date (f) *date*
date de péremption (f) *sell-by date*
date d'expiration (f) *expiration date*
dauphin (m) *dolphin*
de *from; of*
débarquer *to disembark*
début (m) *beginning*
débutant/débutante (m/f) *beginner*

décembre *December*
décoller *to take off (plane)*
déconnecter: se déconnecter (informatique) *to log out*
décontracté/décontractée *casual*
décor (m) *set*
découvert (m) *overdraft*
degrés (m pl) *degrees*
dehors *outside*
déjà *already*
déjeuner (m) *lunch*
délicieux/délicieuse *delicious*
demain *tomorrow*
dent (f) *tooth*
dentifrice (m) *toothpaste*
dentiste (m/f) *dentist*
déodorant (m) *deodorant*
départ (m) *departure*
déposer *to deposit*
dépôt (m) *bus station*
dernier/dernière *last*
derrière *back (not front of); behind*
descendre *to get off*
désert (m) *desert*
désolé/désolée *sorry*
désorienté/désorientée *confused*
dessert (m) *dessert*
dessin (m) *drawing*
dessiner *to draw*
dessous-de-verre (m) *coaster*
destination (f) *destination*
détecteur de fumée (m) *smoke alarm*
détester *to hate*
deux *two*
deuxième *second (position)*
devant *in front of*

développer *to develop (a film)*
devises étrangères (pl) *foreign currency*
devoir *to have to (verb); to owe*
diabétique *diabetic*
diarrhée (f) *diarrhea*
dictionnaire (m) *dictionary*
diésel (m) *diesel*
difficile *difficult*
dimanche *Sunday*
dîner (m) *dinner*
dire *to say; to tell*
direction (f) *direction*
discuter *to discuss*
disquaire (m) *record dealer*
distance (f) *distance*
distributeur (m) *cash machine*
divorcé/divorcée *divorced*
dix *ten*
doigt (m) *finger*
doigt de pied (m) *toe*
donc *so*
donner *to give*
dos (m) *back (body)*
dossier (m) *file*
dossier (m) *back*
douane (f) *customs*
doubler *to pass*
douche (f) *shower*
douleur (f) *pain*
douloureux/douloureuse *sore; painful*
douze *twelve*
drap (m) *sheet*
drapeau (m) *flag*
droit/droite *straight*
droit/droite *right (direction)*
dur/dure *hard*
DVD (m) *DVD*

E
eau (f) *water*
eau de Javel (f) *bleach*
eau en bouteille (f) *bottled water*
eau gazeuse (f) *sparkling/fizzy water*
eau minérale (f) *mineral water*
écharde (f) *splinter*
école (f) *school*
écouter *to listen*
écouteurs (m pl) *headphones*
écran total (m) *sunblock*
écrasé/écrasée *crushed*
écrire *to write*
édulcorant artificiel (m) *artificial sweetener*
effet secondaire (m) *side effect*
effrayé/effrayée *scared*
église (f) *church*
égout (m) *drain*
égratignure (f) *graze (on skin)*
électricien (m) *electrician*
électricité (f) *electricity*
elle *she/it*
e-mail (m) *email*
embarquer *to board*
émigrer *to emigrate*
emporter *to take away*
emprunter *to borrow*
en bas *down*
encaisser *to cash*
en-cas (m) *snack*
enceinte *pregnant*
enchanté/enchantée *pleased to meet you*
encore *again; still*
endommagé/endommagée *damaged*
en-dessous *below; beneath*
enfants (m pl) *children*

en plus extra
enregistrement (m) check in
enregistrement des bagages (m) check-in desk
enregistrer to check in
enseignement supérieur (m) college
ensoleillé/ensoleillée sunny
entendre to hear
entre between
entrée (f) appetizer
entrée (f) entrance
entrée interdite no entry
enveloppe (f) envelope
envoyer to send
épais/épaisse thick
épaule (f) shoulder
épicé/épicée hot (spicy)
épicerie (f) grocer
épices (f pl) spices
épilation (f) wax
épileptique epileptic
épinards (m pl) spinach
éplucher to peel
éplucheur (m) peeler
éponge (f) sponge
épouse (f) wife
épreuve (f) print
épreuve (f) trial; hardship
équipe (f) team
équipement (m) equipment
équitation (f) horseback riding
erreur (f) error
escalade (f) rock climbing
escalier (m) staircase
escalier de secours (m) fire escape
escaliers (m pl) stairs
essai (m) try
essence (f) gasoline

essuie-glaces (m pl) windshield wipers
essuyer to wipe
est (m) east
estomac (m) stomach
et and
étage (m) floor
étagère (f) shelf
États-Unis (m pl) United States
été (m) summer
éteindre to turn off
éternuement (m) sneeze
éternuer to sneeze
étiquette (f) label
étouffer to choke
être to be
étroit/étroite narrow
étudiant/étudiante (m/f) student
étui (m) case
euro (m) euro
évier (m) sink
exactement exactly
examiner to examine
excité/excitée excited
exposition (f) exhibition
expulsion (f) send off
extincteur (m) fire extinguisher

F

fâché/fâchée angry
facile easy
facteur (m) mail carrier
facture (f) invoice
facturer to charge; to invoice
faible weak
faire to do; to make
faire de la voile to go sailing
faire du vélo to go cycling
faire les courses to go shopping

faire marche arrière
    to reverse
faire un paquet-cadeau
    to wrap (a gift)
faire une réservation
    to book
falaise (f) *cliff*
famille (f) *family*
fard à joues (m) *blush*
faux/fausse *false; wrong*
femme (f) *woman*
femme de ménage (f)
    cleaner
fenêtre (f) *window*
fer à repasser (m) *iron*
ferme (f) *farm*
fermé/fermée *closed*
fermer *to close*
fermer à clé *to lock*
fermeture Éclair (f) *zipper*
ferry (m) *ferry*
fête (f) *celebration; party*
fête foraine (f) *funfair*
feux (m pl) *traffic lights*
feux de détresse (m pl)
    hazard lights
février *February*
ficelle (f) *string*
fiche (f) *form*
fier/fière *proud*
fièvre (f) *fever*
filet (m) *fillet*
filet (m) *net*
fille (f) *daughter; girl*
film (m) *movie*
fils (m) *son*
fin (f) *end*
finir *to finish*
flash (m) *flash*
fleur (f) *flower*
fleuriste (f) *florist*
foncé/foncée *dark*
fontaine (f) *fountain*

football (m) *soccer*
forêt (f) *forest*
forêt tropicale (f) *rain forest*
forfait (m) *fixed or set price;*
    package
forfait-skieur(s) (m) *ski-pass*
formalités de départ (f pl)
    check out (of hotel)
forme physique (f) *fitness*
fouet (m) *whisk*
foulard (m) *scarf*
foulure (f) *sprain*
four (m) *oven*
fourchette (f) *fork*
fourre-tout (m) *duffel bag*
fracture (f) *fracture*
fragile *fragile*
frais bancaires (m pl) *bank charge*
frais/fraîche *fresh*
fraise (f) *strawberry*
framboise (f) *raspberry*
français/française *French*
franchise de bagages (f)
    baggage allowance
frein (m) *brake*
frère (m) *brother*
friandise (f) *snack bar*
frigo (m) *refrigerator*
frire *to fry*
frisé/frisée *curly*
frit/frite *fried*
frites *French fries*
froid/froide *cold*
fromage (m) *cheese*
fruits (m pl) *fruit*
fruits de mer (m pl) *seafood*
fuite (f) *leak*
fumer *to smoke*

G

gagner *to win*
galerie (f) *galley*
galerie (f) *roofrack*

galerie d'art (f) *art gallery*
gants (m pl) *gloves*
gants de cuisine (m pl)
  oven mitts
garage (m) *garage*
garantie (f) *guarantee*
garçon (m) *boy*
garde d'enfants (f) *babysitting*
garde-côte (m) *coast guard*
garder *to keep*
gare (f) *train/bus station*
gâteau (m) *cake*
gauche (f) *left (direction)*
gaz (m) *gas*
gazole (m) *diesel*
gel (m) *frost*
gel douche (m) *shower gel*
gêné/gênée *embarrassed*
genou (m) *knee*
gens (m pl) *people*
gilet (m) *cardigan*
gilet de sauvetage (m) *life jacket*
gingembre (m) *ginger*
girafe (f) *giraffe*
givre (m) *frost*
glace (f) *ice; ice cream*
glacière (f) *cooler*
glaçon (m) *ice cube*
golf (m) *golf*
gorge (f) *throat*
GPS (m) *GPS receiver*
grain de beauté (m)
  mole (medical)
graines (f pl) *seeds*
grains (m pl) *beans (e.g. coffee)*
gramme (m) *gram*
grand/grande *big*
grand magasin (m)
  department store
Grande-Bretagne (f)
  Great Britain
gras (m) *fat*
gratuit/gratuite *free (no charge)*

grave *serious*
grêle (f) *hail*
grille-pain (m) *toaster*
griller *to broil*
grippe (f) *flu*
gris/grise *gray*
groupe (m) *group*
guichet (m) *ticket office*
guichet automatique (m)
  automatic ticket machine
guide (m) *guide; guidebook*
guide audio (m) *audio guide*
guêpe (f) *wasp*
gym (f) *gym*

H

habituel/habituelle *usual*
hall de gare (m)
  station concourse
hamburger (m) *burger*
hanche (f) *hip*
handicapé/handicapée (m/f)
  disabled person
haut: en haut *up*
hauteur (f) *height*
herbe (f) *herb*
heure (f) *hour; time*
heures d'ouverture (f pl)
  opening times
heureux/heureuse *happy*
hier *yesterday*
hiver (m) *winter*
hockey (m) *hockey*
homme (m) *man*
hôpital (m) *hospital*
horaires (m pl) *timetable*
horaires de visite (m pl)
  visiting hours
horaires d'ouverture (m pl)
  opening hours
horloge (f) *clock*
horodateur (m) *parking meter*
hors-jeu *off-side*

hôte (m) *host*
hôte (m) *guest*
hôtel (m) *hotel*
hôtesse de l'air (f) *air stewardess*
huile de tournesol (f) *sunflower oil*
huile d'olive (f) *olive oil*
huit *eight*
humide *humid*
hydroglisseur (m) *hydrofoil*

I

ici *here*
il *he/it*
île (f) *island*
il y a *there is/are*
immeuble (m) *apartment building*
immigration (f) *immigration*
imperméable (m) *raincoat*
impôt (m) *tax*
imprimer *to print*
incendie (m) *fire*
infection (f) *infection*
infirmier/infirmière (m/f) *nurse*
information (f) *information*
inhalateur (m) *inhaler*
inondation (f) *flood*
inquiet/inquiète *worried*
insectifuge (m) *insect repellent*
intéressant/intéressante *interesting*
internet (m) *internet*
interrupteur (m) *switch*
inventaire (m) *inventory*
invité/invitée (m/f) *guest*

J

jamais *never*
jambe (f) *leg*
janvier *January*

jardin (m) *garden*
jaune *yellow*
je *I (first person)*
jean (m) *jeans*
jeton (m) *counter*
jeu (m) *game*
jeu de cartes (m) *pack of cards*
jeu vidéo (m) *video game*
jeudi *Thursday*
jeune *young*
joli/-joliee *nice; pretty*
jonc (m) *rush*
joue (f) *cheek*
jouer *to play*
jouet (m) *toy*
jour (m) *day*
jour férié (m) *public holiday*
journal (m) *newspaper*
juillet *July*
juin *June*
jupe (f) *skirt*
jus (m) *juice*
jus de pomme (m) *apple juice*
jus d'orange (m) *orange juice*
jusqu'à *until*
juste *correct*

K

kayak (m) *kayak*
kilo (m) *kilo*
kilogramme (m) *kilogram*
kilomètre (m) *kilometer*
Klaxon (m) *horn*
Kleenex (m) *tissue*

L

là *there*
là-bas *over there*
lac (m) *lake*
lâcher *to release*
laid/laide *ugly*

laine (f) *wool*
laisser tremper *to soak*
lait (m) *milk*
lait corporel (m) *body lotion*
laitue (f) *lettuce*
lampe torche (f) *flashlight*
langue (f) *tongue*
lapin (m) *rabbit*
large *wide*
largeur (f) *width*
lavabo (m) *sink*
lave-auto (m) *car wash*
lave-linge (m) *washing machine*
lave-vaisselle (m) *dishwasher*
laver *to wash*
laverie automatique (f)
    laundromat
lecteur de DVD (m) *DVD player*
léger/légère *light*
légume (m) *vegetable*
lent/lente *slow*
lentilles (f pl) *lentils*
lentilles de contact (f pl)
    contact lenses
lequel? *which?*
leur/leurs *their*
lever du soleil (m) *sunrise*
levier de vitesses (m)
    gear shift
librairie (f) *bookstore*
libre *free (not occupied)*
ligne (f) *line*
  en ligne *online*
limonade (f) *lemonade*
lingette (f) *wipe*
liquide (m) *cash*
liquide (m) *liquid*
lire *to read*
liste (f) *list*
lit de bronzage (m) *bed*
lit à deux places (m)
    double bed
lit enfants (m) *crib*

lit simple (m) *single bed*
lit à U.V. (m) *sunbed*
liter (m) *litre*
lits jumeaux (m pl) *twin beds*
livre (f) *pound*
livre (m) *book*
local/locale *local*
location de voiture (f)
    car rental
logement (m) *accommodation*
loin *far*
loisirs (m pl) *leisure activities;*
    hobbies
long/longue *long*
longueur (f) *length*
louer *to hire; to rent*
lourd/lourde *heavy*
lui *him*
lumière (f) *light (noun)*
lundi *Monday*
lunettes (f pl) *glasses; goggles*
lunettes de soleil (f pl)
    sunglasses

M

machine (f) *machine*
mâchoire (f) *jaw*
maçon (m) *construction worker*
magasin (m) *store*
magasin de chaussures (m)
    shoe store
magasin de meubles (m)
    furniture store
magasin hors taxe (m)
    duty-free store
magazine (m) *magazine*
mai *May*
maillet (m) *mallet*
maillot de bain (m) *swimsuit*
main (f) *hand*
maintenant *now*
mairie (f) *town hall*
maïs (m) *corn*

maison (f) *house*
mal *bad*
mal au ventre (m) *stomach ache*
mal de dents (m) *toothache*
mal de tête (m) *headache*
malade *ill*
maladie (f) *illness*
mallette (f) *briefcase*
manège (m) *merry-go-round;*
   riding school
manger *to eat*
manger sur place *eat-in*
mangue (f) *mango*
manicure (f) *manicure*
manteau (m) *coat*
manuel (m) *manual*
manuscript (m) *manuscript*
maquillage (m) *makeup*
marché (m) *market*
marcher *to walk*
mardi *Tuesday*
marée (f) *tide*
mari (m) *husband*
mariage (m) *wedding*
marié/mariée *married*
marmite (f) *casserole dish*
marron *brown*
mars *March*
mascara (m) *mascara*
massage (m) *massage*
mat/mate *matte*
match (m) *game;*
   match (sport)
matelas (m) *mattress*
matin (m) *morning*
mayonnaise (f) *mayonnaise*
me *me; myself*
mécanicien/mécanicienne (m/f)
   mechanic
médecin (m) *doctor*
médicament pour la toux (m)
   cough medicine
médicaments (m pl) *medicine*

méduse (f) *jellyfish*
même *same*
menottes (f pl) *handcuffs*
menthe (f) *mint*
menton (m) *chin*
menu (m) *menu*
menu du déjeuner (m)
   lunch menu
menu du soir (m)
   evening menu
mer (f) *sea*
Merci *thank you*
mercredi *Wednesday*
mère (f) *mother*
message (m) *message*
message vocal (m) *voice*
   message
mesure (f) *measure*
métal (m) *metal*
mètre (m) *meter*
métro (m) *subway*
mettre *to put*
micro-ondes (m) *microwave*
midi *noon*
mieux *better*
migraine (f) *migraine*
milieu (m) *middle*
mince *thin*
mini bar (m) *mini bar*
minuit *midnight*
minute (f) *minute*
miroir (m) *mirror*
mode (f) *fashion*
mode d'emploi (m) *instructions*
moi *me*
mois (m) *month*
moitié (f) *half*
mon/ma/mes *my*
montagne (f) *mountain*
montant (m) *amount*
monter une tente *to pitch a tent*
montre (f) *watch*
monument (m) *monument*

morceau (m) *piece; bit*
morsure (f) *bite*
   (e.g. from an animal)
morue (f) *cod*
moteur (m) *engine*
moto (f) *motorcycle*
mou/molle *soft*
mouillé/mouillée *wet*
moulu/moulue *ground*
mousse à raser (f)
   shaving foam
moustiquaire (f)
   mosquito net
moustique (m) *mosquito*
moutarde (f) *mustard*
moyen/moyenne *medium*
mozzarella (f) *mozzarella*
mur (m) *wall*
mûr/mûre *ripe*
mûre (f) *blackberry*
muscle (m) *muscle*
musée (m) *museum*
musicien/musicienne (m/f)
   musician
musique (f) *music*
myrtille (f) *blueberry*

N

nager *to swim*
naissance (f) *birth*
nausée (f) *nausea*
navigation par satellite (f)
   satellite navigation
naviguer *to browse (internet)*
naviguer *to navigate*
ne... pas *don't*
neiger *to snow*
nerveux/nerveuse *nervous*
neuf *nine*
nez (m) *nose*
noir/noire *black*
noix (f pl) *walnuts*
noix de coco (f) *coconut*

nom (m) *name*
non *no*
nord (m) *north*
normal/normale *normal*
nos (pl) *our*
note (f) *bill; note*
notre *our*
nourriture (f) *food*
nous *we*
nouveau/nouvelle *new*
nouvelles (f pl) *news*
novembre *November*
nuage (m) *cloud*
nuageux/nuageuse *cloudy*
nuit (f) *night*
numéro à contacter (m)
   contact number
numéro de compte (m)
   account number
numéro de vol (m)
   flight number

O

objectif (m) *(camera) lens*
objets de valeur (m pl)
   valuables
objets trouvés (m pl)
   lost property
obtenir *to get; to obtain*
occupé/occupée *engaged/busy*
océan (m) *ocean*
octobre *October*
œil (m) *eye*
œuf (m) *egg*
office du tourisme (m)
   tourist information office
oignon (m) *onion*
oiseau (m) *bird*
olives (f pl) *olives*
omelette (f) *omelet*
oncle (m) *uncle*
ongle (m) *nail*
onze *eleven*

opéra (m) *opera*
opération (f) *operation*
or (m) *gold*
orange (f) *orange*
orchestre (m) *orchestra*
ordinateur (m) *computer*
ordinateur portable (m)
  laptop
ordonnance (f) *prescription*
ordre (m) *order*
oreille (f) *ear*
oreiller (m) *pillow*
orteil (m) *toe*
ou *or*
où? *where?*
oublier *to forget*
ouest (m) *west*
oui *yes*
ouragan (m) *hurricane*
ours (m) *bear*
ouvert/ouverte *open*
ouvre-boîtes (m) *can opener*
ouvre-bouteilles (m)
  bottle opener
ouvrir *to open*

P

paiement (m) *payment*
pain (m) *bread*
pain bis (m) *whole-wheat bread*
paire (f) *pair*
palmes (f pl) *fins*
panier (m) *basket*
panier de pique-nique (m)
  picnic hamper
panne (f) *breakdown*
panneau (m) *signpost*
panneau d'affichage (m)
  bulletin board
panneau de signalisation (m)
  street sign
panneaux routiers (m pl)
  road signs

pansement (m) *adhesive bandage*
pantalon (m) *pants*
pantoufles (f pl) *slippers*
papier (m) *paper*
papier-cadeau (m)
  wrapping paper
papiers d'identité (m pl)
  identity papers
paquet (m) *package;*
  packet; parcel
par *by; through*
parapluie (m) *umbrella*
parasol (m) *beach umbrella*
parc (m) *park*
parc d'attractions (m)
  amusement park
parc national (m) *national park*
parcmètre (m)
  parking meter
pardon *excuse me; sorry*
pare-brise (m) *windshield*
pare-choc (m) *bumper*
parents (m pl) *parents;*
  relatives
parfum (m) *perfume*
parking (m) *parking lot; parking*
parler *to speak; to talk*
parmesan (m) *Parmesan*
part (f) *piece; slice*
partenaire (m/f) *partner*
partir *to depart; to leave;*
  to go
partition (musique) (f)
  score; sheet music
pas *not*
pas (m) *step*
passage (m) *alleyway;*
  path; crossing
passage piétons (m)
  pedestrian crossing
passager/passagère (m/f)
  passenger
passe (f) *pass*

passeport (m) *passport*
passer: se passer *to happen*
passoire (f) *colander*
pastèque (f) *watermelon*
pastille pour la gorge (f)
  throat lozenge
patate douce (f) *sweet potato*
pâte (f) *pastry*
pâtes (f pl) *pasta*
patient/patiente (m/f) *patient*
patin à glace (m) *skate*
patinage (m) *ice-skating*
pâtisserie (f) *pastry*
pause (f) *pause*
payer *to pay*
pays (m) *country*
péage (m) *toll*
peau (f) *skin*
pêche (f) *fishing*
pêche (f) *peach*
pédicure (f) *pedicure*
peigne (m) *comb*
peinture (f) *painting*
pelle (f) *shovel; dust pan*
pellicule (f) *film (camera)*
peluche (f) *stuffed animal*
pendant *during*
penser *to think*
pente (f) *slope*
percolateur (m) *coffee machine*
perdre *to lose*
père (m) *father*
permis de conduire (m)
  driver's license
persil (m) *parsley*
personne âgée (f)
  senior citizen
personnel (m) *staff*
peser *to weigh*
petit/petite *little*
petite assiette (f) *side plate*
petit-déjeuner (m) *breakfast*
peut-être *perhaps*

phare (m) *headlight;*
  lighthouse
pharmacie (f) *pharmacy*
pharmacien/pharmacienne (m/f)
  pharmacist
photo (f) *photograph*
photocopier *to copy*
photographier *to photograph*
pianiste (m/f) *pianist*
pichet (m) *jug*
pièce (f) *coin*
pièce (f) *part*
pièce (f) *room (in house)*
pièce de théâtre (f) *play*
pièce d'identité (f) *ID*
pièce jointe (f) *attachment*
pied (m) *foot*
pierre (f) *stone*
pierre précieuse (f)
  precious stone
pieuvre (f) *octopus*
pilote (m) *pilot*
pilule (f) *pill*
piment (m) *chilli pepper*
pince à épiler (f) *tweezers*
pinceau (m) *paint brush*
pique-nique (m) *picnic*
piquet (m) *tent peg*
piqûre (f) *injection*
piqûre (f) *sting (insect; nettle; etc.)*
pire *worse*
piscine (f) *swimming pool*
piste cyclable (f) *cycle lane*
piste verte (f) *green slope (skiing)*
pizza (f) *pizza*
place (f) *place; square*
  (in town); vacancy
place de couloir (f) *aisle seat*
place de parking
  réservée aux handicapés (f)
  disabled parking
plafond (m) *ceiling*
plage (f) *beach*

plainte (f) *complaint*
plan (m) *map*
plan de métro (m)
  subway map
planche à découper (f)
  cutting board
planche à repasser (f)
  ironing board
planche à voile (f) *windsurf board*
planche de surf (f) *surfboard*
planète (f) *planet*
plantes (f pl) *plants*
plaque de cuisson (f) *cookie sheet*
plaque d'immatriculation (f)
  vehicle registration plate
plaques rouges (f pl) *rash*
plat (m) *dish; course*
plat d'accompagnement (m)
  side dish
plat principal (m)
  main course
plateau (m) *tray*
plein/pleine *full*
pleurer *to cry*
pleuvoir *to rain*
plombier (m) *plumber*
plongée (f) *scuba diving*
plongeon (m) *dive*
plonger *to dive*
plus *more*
pneu (m) *tire*
pneu crevé (m) *puncture*
poche (f) *pocket*
poêle (f) *frying pan*
poids (m) *weight*
poids maximum autorisé (m)
  weight allowance
poignée (f) *handle*
poignet (m) *wrist*
point (m) *point*
pointe (f) *tip*
pointure (f) *shoe size*
poire (f) *pear*

pois chiches (m pl) *chickpeas*
poisson (m) *fish*
poissonier (m) *fish seller*
poitrine (f) *chest*
poivre (m) *pepper*
poivron (m) *pepper*
police (f) *police*
police d'assurance (f)
  insurance policy
policier/policière (m/f)
  police officer
pommade (f) *ointment*
pomme (f) *apple*
pomme de terre (f) *potato*
pompe (f) *pump*
pompiers (m pl) *fire department*
porc (m) *pork*
port (m) *harbor*
port de plaisance (m)
  marina
porte (f) *door; gate*
porte-bagages (m)
  luggage rack
porte d'embarquement (f)
  boarding gate
porte d'entrée (f) *front door*
porte-manteau (m)
  coat hanger
porte-monnaie (m) *change purse*
portefeuille (m) *wallet*
porter *to carry*
porter plainte *to complain*
porteur (m) *porter*
portiere (f) *door (of car)*
portillon (m) *ticket gate*
portion (f) *portion*
posologie (f) *dosage*
possible *possible*
poste (f) *post office*
poster *to mail*
pot (m) *jar; jug; tub*
pot d'échappement (m)
  car exhaust

poubelle (f) *trash can; garbage can*
pouce (m) *thumb*
poudre (f) *powder*
poulet (m) *chicken*
poupée (f) *doll*
pour *for*
pour affaires *on business*
pourquoi? *why?*
poussez *push*
pouvoir *to be able to*
préféré/préférée *favorite*
préférer *to prefer*
prélèvement (m) *automatic payment*
premier/première *first*
premier étage (m) *second floor*
premiers secours (m pl) *first aid*
prendre *to take*
prendre le train *to go by train*
prendre l'avion *to fly*
prendre un bain de soleil *to sunbathe*
près de *near; next to*
préservatif (m) *condom*
presque *almost*
presse (f) *press*
pressé/pressée *in a hurry*
pression artérielle (f) *blood pressure*
pression des pneus (f) *tire pressure*
prêt (m) *loan*
prêt/prête *ready*
printemps (m) *spring*
prise (électrique) (f) *plug*
prix (m) *fare; price*
problème cardiaque (m) *heart condition*
prochain/prochaine *next*

proche *nearby*
programme (m) *program*
projection (f) *projection; screening*
propre *clean*
prospectus (m) *leaflet*
province (f) *province*
provisions (f pl) *groceries*
prudence (f) *caution*
prune (f) *plum*
public (m) *audience*
pull (m) *jumper*
pyjama (m) *pajamas*

Q

quai (m) *platform*
quand *when*
quarante *forty*
quart (m) *quarter*
quatre *four*
que *than; that*
quelque chose *something*
quelquefois *sometimes*
quelques *some*
quelqu'un *someone; somebody*
quincaillerie (f) *hardware store*
quinze jours *fortnight*
quitter *to leave*
quoi? *what?*

R

rabot (m) *plane (carpentry)*
racine (f) *root*
radiateur (m) *radiator*
radio (f) *radio; X-ray*
radio numérique (f) *digital radio*
radio-réveil (m) *clock radio*
ragoût (m) *stew*
rail (m) *rail*

ralentir *slow down*

rallonge (f) *extension cord*

rame (f) *oar*

rameur (m) *rowing machine*

rampe d'accès handicapés (f) *wheelchair ramp*

randonnée (f) *hike; hiking*

rangée (f) *row*

râpe (f) *grater*

raquette de tennis (f) *tennis racket*

rarement *rarely*

raser: se raser *to shave*

rasoir (m) *razor*

rasoir électrique (m) *electric razor*

rat (m) *rat*

rayon (m) *spoke*

réanimation (f) *resuscitation*

réception (f) *reception*

réceptionniste (m/f) *receptionist*

recevoir *to receive*

réchaud (m) *camping stove*

recherche (f) *research*

récif de corail (m) *coral reef*

récipient (m) *container*

recommander *to recommend*

record (m) *record (sport)*

reçu (m) *receipt*

redémarrer *to restart; to reboot*

réduction (f) *reduction*

réfrigérateur (m) *refrigerator*

refroidissement (m) *chill*

regarder *to look; to watch*

région (f) *region*

rein (m) *kidney*

remercier *to thank*

remorquer *to tow*

remplacer *to replace*

remplir *to fill*

remuer *to stir*

rendez-vous (m) *appointment*

renverser *to knock down; to knock over; to spill*

réparer *to fix; to mend; to repair*

repas (m) *meal*

répondeur (m) *answering machine*

répondre *to answer*

requin (m) *shark*

réseau (m) *network*

réservation (f) *reservation*

réserver *to book; to reserve*

réservoir (m) *tank*

réservoir d'essence (m) *fuel gauge*

restaurant (m) *restaurant*

restauration rapide (f) *fast food*

rester *to stay; to be left*

retard: en retard *late*

retour (m) *return*

retrait (m) *withdrawal (of money)*

retraité/retraitée *retired*

réveil (m) *alarm clock*

réveil par téléphone (m) *wake-up call*

rhume (m) *cold (illness)*

rhume des foins (m) *hay fever*

rideau (m) *curtain*

rien *nothing*

rincer *to rinse*

rire *to laugh*

rivière (f) *river*

riz (m) *rice*

riz complet (m) *brown rice*

robe (f) *dress*

robe de soirée (f) *evening dress*

robinet (m) *faucet*

rocher (m) *rock*
rond/ronde *round*
rond-point (m) *traffic circle*
ronfler *to snore*
rose *pink*
rôti (m) *roast*
roue (f) *wheel*
roue de secours (f) *spare tire*
rouge *red*
rouleau de papier hygiénique (m)
   toilet papers
route (f) *road*
rubis (m) *ruby*

S

sable (m) *sand*
sac (m) *bag*
sac à main (m) *handbag*
sac de couchage (m)
   sleeping bag
sac fourre-tout (m) *holdall*
sachet de thé (m) *teabag*
saignement (m) *bleeding*
saignement de nez (m)
   nosebleed
saison (f) *season*
salade (f) *salad*
salami (m) *salami*
sale *dirty*
salé/salée *salted; savory*
salle à manger (f)
   dining room
salle d'attente (f)
   waiting room
salle de bain (f) *bathroom*
salle de départ (f)
   departure lounge
salle des urgences (f)
   emergency room
salon (m) *living room*
salon de coiffure (m)
   hairdresser's
salut *hello*

samedi *Saturday*
sandale (f) *sandal*
sans *without*
sans pépins *seedless*
santé (f) *health*
Santé! *Cheers!*
sauce (f) *sauce*
saucisse (f) *sausage*
saumon (m) *salmon*
sauna (m) *sauna*
sauté/sautée *pan fried*
sauter *to sauté*
sauver *to save*
sauveteur (m) *lifeguard*
savoir *to know (a fact)*
savon (m) *soap*
scanner (m) *scan*
scarabée (m) *beetle*
scène (f) *stage; scene*
scooter (m) *scooter*
Scotch (m) *adhesive tape*
seau (m) *bucket; pail*
sec/sèche *dry*
sèche-cheveux (m) *blow-dryer*
sèche-linge (m) *tumble dryer*
sécher *to dry*
seconde (f) *second (time)*
securité: en sécurité *safe*
sel (m) *salt*
semaine (f) *week*
sembler *to look; to appear*
s'ennuyer *to be bored*
sensible *sensitive*
sentier (m) *footpath*
sentir: se sentir *to feel*
séparément *separately*
sept *seven*
septembre *September*
se réveiller *to wake up*
serpent (m) *snake*
serpillère (f) *mop*
serré/serrée *tight*
serveur (m) *server; waiter*

serveuse (f) *server; waitress*
service (m) *service*
service en chambre (m)
    room service
service rapide (m)
    express service
services d'urgence (m pl)
    emergency services
serviette (f) *napkin; towel*
serviette de bain (f)
    bath towel
serviette de plage (f)
    beach towel
serviette hygiénique (f)
    sanitary napkin
servir *to serve*
seul/seule *alone*
seulement *only*
s'évanouir *to faint*
shampooing (m) *shampoo*
short (m) *shorts*
si *so; if*
siège (m) *seat*
siège enfant (m) *child seat*
signal (m) *signal*
signature (f) *signature*
signer *to sign*
silence (m) *rest*
singe (m) *monkey*
sirène (f) *siren*
site web (m) *website*
six *six*
ski (m) *ski*
ski nautique (m)
    waterskiing
skier *to ski*
slip (m) *briefs*
smartphone (m)
    smartphone
SMS (m) *text (SMS)*
snowboard (m) *snowboard*
société (f) *company*
soda (m) *soda water*

sœur (f) *sister*
soie (f) *silk*
soins de bébés (m pl)
    baby changing room
soir (m) *evening*
sol (m) *floor*
sol (m) *soil*
soleil (m) *sun; sunshine*
somnifère (m) *sleeping pill*
sonnette (f) *(door) bell*
sorbet (m) *sherbet*
sortie (f) *exit*
sortie de secours (f)
    emergency exit
sortir *to go out*
sortir en boîte *to go
    to clubs*
sortir manger *to eat out*
soucoupe (f) *saucer*
soupe (f) *soup*
sourcil (m) *eyebrow*
sourire (m) *smile*
souris (f) *mouse (computer)*
souris (f) *mouse*
sous *under*
sous-sol (m) *basement*
sous-vêtements (m pl)
    underwear
souvenir (m) *souvenir*
souvent *often*
spatule (f) *spatula*
spécialité (f) *speciality*
sport (m) *sport*
sports aquatiques (m pl)
    watersports
sports d'hiver (m pl)
    winter sports
station de métro (f)
    subway station
station de taxis (f)
    taxi stand
station-service (f)
    gas station

statue (f) *statue*
store (m) *Venetian blind*
stress (m) *stress*
stylo (m) *pen*
sucré/sucrée *sweet*
sud (m) *south*
supermarché (m)
   supermarket
support (m) *rack; stand; support*
suppositoires (m pl)
   suppositories
sur *on*
surf des neiges (m)
   snowboarding
surfer *to surf*
surgelé *frozen*
surpris *surprised*
sweat-shirt (m) *sweatshirt*

T

tabac (m) *tobaccos*
tabac-presse (m) *newsstand*
table (f) *table*
table basse (f) *coffee table*
tableau (m) *board*
tableau des départs (m)
   departure board
tablier (m) *apron*
taille (f) *clothes size*
tailleur (m) *tailor*
talon (m) *heel*
tampon (m) *tampon*
tante (f) *aunt*
tapis (m) *carpet*
tard *late*
tarif (m) *price list*
tarif d'affranchissement (m)
   postage
tarte (f) *tart*
tasse (f) *cup*
tasse à café (f) *coffee cup*
taux de change (m)
   exchange rate

taxi (m) *taxi*
télé satellite (f) *satellite TV*
télécharger *to download*
télécommande (f)
   remote control
téléphérique (m) *cable car*
téléphone (m) *telephone*
téléphone portable (m)
   cell phone
téléphone public (m)
   payphone
téléphoner *to phone*
télésiège (m) *chair lift*
téléviseur grand écran (m)
   widecreen TV
télévision (f) *television*
télévision par câble (f)
   cable television
temps (m) *time*
temps (m) *weather*
temps libre (m) *leisure*
température (f)
   temperature
tempête (f) *storm*
tenir *to hold*
tennis (m) *tennis*
tennis (m pl) *sneakers*
tente (f) *tent*
terminal (m) *terminal*
terminé/terminée *finished*
terrain de camping (m)
   campsite
terrain de foot/cricket (m)
   soccer/cricket pitch
terrain de golf (m)
   golf course
terrain de jeux (m)
   playground
terrain pour caravanes (m)
   camper van site
test de grossesse (m)
   pregnancy test
tête (f) *head*

TGV (m) *high-speed train*
thé (m) *tea*
théâtre (m) *theater*
théière (f) *teapot*
thé noir (m) *black tea*
thé vert (m) *green tea*
thermomètre (m) *thermometer*
thermostat (m) *thermostat*
thon (m) *tuna*
ticket (m) *ticket*
tilleul (m) *lime*
timbre (m) *stamp*
timide *shy*
tire-bouchon (m) *corkscrew*
tiroir (m) *drawer*
tissu (m) *fabric*
toboggan (m) *slide*
toi *you*
toilettes (f pl) *restrooms*
toit (m) *roof*
tomate (f) *tomato*
tomate cerise (f) *cherry tomato*
ton/ta/tes *your*
tongs (f pl) *flip-flops*
tôt *early*
toujours *always*
tour (m) *tour*
tour en bateau (m) *boat trip*
tourisme (m) *sightseeing*
touriste (m) *tourist*
tourner *to turn*
tourte (f) *pie*
tout *all*
toux (f) *cough*
train (m) *train*
tramway (m) *tram*
tranche (f) *slice*
transat (m) *deck chair*
transport (m) *transportation*

travail (m) *work*
travailler *to work*
travaux (m pl) *roadwork*
travers: à travers *through*
traversée (f) *crossing*
traverser *to cross*
tremblement de terre (m) *earthquake*
trente *thirty*
trépied (m) *tripod*
tricot de corps (m) *undershirt*
triste *sad*
trognon (m) *core*
trois *three*
trottoir (m) *sidewalk*
trousse de premiers secours (f) *first-aid box*
trouver *to find*
truite (f) *trout*
tu *you*
tuba (m) *snorkel*
tube (m) *tube*

U

un/une *one*
un peu *a little*
uniforme (m) *uniform*
unité de soins intensifs (f) *intensive care unit*
université (f) *college*
urgence (f) *emergency*
urgences (f pl) *accident and emergency department*
urgent *urgent*
utile *useful*
utiliser *to use*

V

vacances (f pl) *vacation*
vache (f) *cow*
vague (f) *wave*
vaisselle (f) *dishes*
valeur (f) *value*

valider to validate
valise (f) suitcase
vapeur: à la vapeur
  steamed
vaporisateur (m) spray
végétarien/végétarienne
  vegetarian
véhicule (m) vehicle
vélo (m) bicycle
vélo de ville (m) road bike
vélo d'appartement (m)
  exercise bike
vendeur/vendeuse (m/f)
  sales assistant
vendredi Friday
venir to come
vent (m) wind
ventilateur (m) fan
verglacé/verglacée icy
verglas (m) ice (on the road)
verre (m) glass
verre à vin (m) wine glass
vers towards
verser to pay in
verser to pour
vert/verte green
veste (f) jacket
vestiaire (m) cloakroom;
  fitting room
vêtements (m pl)
  clothes
vétérinaire (m/f)
  veterinarian
viande (f) meat
vide empty
vider to empty;
  to vacate
vieux/vielle old
vignoble (m) vineyard
village (m) village
ville (f) city; town
vin (m) wine
vinaigre (m) vinegar

vingt twenty
viol (m) rape
violet/violette
  purple
virement bancaire (m)
  bank transfer
virus (m) virus
visa (m) visa
visage (m) face
visite de contrôle (f)
  checkup
visite guidée (f)
  guided tour
visiteur/visiteuse (m/f)
  visitor
vitamine (f)
  vitamin
vite fast; quickly
voie d'accès (f)
  sliproad
voie ferrée (f) (railroad)
  track
voiture (f) car
vol (m) robbery
volaille (f) poultry
volant (m)
  steering wheel
volé/volée stolen
voler to fly
voler to rob
volume (m) volume
vomir to vomit
vos (pl) your
votre your
vouloir to want
vous you
voyage (m) trip
voyager to travel
vrai/vraie right (correct)
vraiment really
VTT (m)
  mountain bike
vue (f) view

W

wagon-restaurant (m) *dining car*
week-end (m) *weekend*
whisky (m) *whiskey*
wifi (m) *Wi-Fi*

Y

yacht (m) *yacht*
yaourt (m) *yogurt*
yoga (m) *yoga*

Z

zéro *zero*
zone (f) *zone*
zone fumeur (f) *smoking area*
zoo (m) *zoo*

ACKNOWLEDGMENTS

ORIGINAL EDITION

Senior Editors Simon Tuite, Angela Wilkes
Editorial Assistant Megan Jones
US Editor Margaret Parrish
Senior Art Editor Vicky Short
Art Editor Mandy Earey
Production Editor Phil Sergeant
Production Controller Inderjit Bhullar
Managing Editor Julie Oughton
Managing Art Editor Louise Dick
Art Director Bryn Walls
Associate Publisher Liz Wheeler
Publisher Jonathan Metcalf

Produced for Dorling Kindersley by SP Creative Design
Editor Heather Thomas
Designer Rolando Ugolino
Language content for Dorling Kindersley by First Edition Translations Ltd
Translator Emmanuelle Rivière
Editor Delphine Clavel
Typesetting Essential Typesetting

Dorling Kindersley would also like to thank the following for their help in the preparation of the original and revised editions of this book: Isabelle Elkaim and Melanie Fitzgerald of First Edition Translations Ltd; Elma Aquino, Mandy Earey, and Meenal Goel for design assistance; Amelia Collins, Nicola Hodgson, Isha Sharma, Janashree Singha, Nishtha Kapil, and Neha Ruth Samuel for editorial assistance; Claire Bowers, Lucy Claxton, and Rose Horridge in the DK Picture Library; Adam Brackenbury, Vânia Cunha, Almudena Diaz, Maria Elia, John Goldsmid, Sonia Pati, Phil Sergeant, and Louise Waller for DTP assistance.

PICTURE CREDITS

The publisher would like to thank the following for their kind permission to reproduce their photographs:
Key: a (above); b (below/bottom); c (centre); l (left); r (right); t (top)
Alamy Images: Justin Kase p113 cb; Martin Lee p52 tr; Photospin, Inc p38 crb;
Alamy Stock Photo: Cultura RM p51br; **Courtesy of Renault:** p26–27 t; **Getty Images:** Reggie Casagrande p148; **PunchStock:** Moodboard p8; **Robert Harding Picture Library:** Ellen Rooney p4; **123RF.com:** Cobalt p108 cr; Norman Kin Hang Chan / Bedo p109 clb; Cobalt p134 bl; Cobalt p156 br

All other images © **Dorling Kindersley**
For further information, see: **www.dkimages.com**

NUMBERS

1 un/une *uhn/ewn*	**7** sept *sayt*	**13** treize *trayz*	**19** dix-neuf *deesnuhf*	**70** soixante-dix *swasohnt-dees*
2 deux *duh*	**8** huit *weet*	**14** quartorze *katorz*	**20** vingt *vahn*	**80** quatre-vingts *katruh-vahn*
3 trois *trwa*	**9** neuf *nuhf*	**15** quinze *kahnz*	**30** trente *trohnt*	**90** quatre-vingt-dix *katruh-vahn-dees*
4 quatre *katruh*	**10** dix *dees*	**16** seize *sayz*	**40** quarante *karohnt*	**100** cent *sohn*
5 cinq *sahnk*	**11** onze *ohnz*	**17** dix-sept *deesayt*	**50** cinquante *sahnkohnt*	**500** cinq cents *sahnk sohn*
6 six *sees*	**12** douze *dooz*	**18** dix-huit *deezweet*	**60** soixante *swasohnt*	**1000** mille *meel*	**10,000** dix mille *dee meel*

ORDINAL NUMBERS

first premier/premiere *pruhmyay/pruhmyair*	**fourth** quatrieme *katreeyaym*	**seventh** septieme *saytyaym*	**tenth** dixieme *deezyaym*
second deuxieme *duhzyaym*	**fifth** cinquieme *sahnkyaym*	**eighth** huiteme *weetyaym*	**twentieth** vingtieme *vahntyaym*
third troisieme *trwazyaym*	**sixth** sixieme *seezyaym*	**ninth** neuvieme *nuhvyaym*	